Terrian Journals presents:

An Adult Book About Education

failures, successes, &
de-schooling night courses

By Donald Murray Anderson

An Adult Book About Education
A Mythbreaker Book
First Edition
© Copyright 2019 by Donald Murray Anderson

ISBN 978-1-989593-03-5

All rights reserved. Without limiting rights under copyright reserved above, no part of this book may be reproduced, stored in or introduced into a retrieval system, or transmitted in any form or by any means (electronic, mechanical, photocopying, recording, or otherwise) without prior written permission of the copyright owner.

For information address: mythbreaker@mail.com

Adult learners are the essential prerequisites, required core content, and most significant evaluation instruments of adult education.

THE CONTINUING EDUCATION OF
AN ADULT LEARNER'S CHILD:
DEDICATION & CONTEXTS

My dad is the first adult learner I know. During my late childhood he decides to try to complete the formal education that he doesn't finish when he's younger.

But this isn't his first or last adult education experience.

At age 20 he completes a correspondence course on writing offered by the Newspaper Institute of America.

In the later years of his life he says he's also interested in going to university and studying science when he's a young person.

But his older brother Lorne is then already at university studying engineering and the family only has enough money to send one of its seven children to university.

Fortunately for my dad, when he gets his first job not having a more advanced formal education doesn't seem to be an obstacle to hiring or advancement for most people.

His young adulthood and job search coincide with the final years of a very severe worldwide financial collapse called "The Great Depression".

Fortunately for my dad, it's nearly ten years since the beginning of that economic disaster and employment opportunities are beginning to return.

In that era, much like later times, employers seem to have little understanding and appreciation of the value of formal education that is not specifically designed entirely and exclusively for "employee training".

Job preparation is later the reason that employers give for hiring community college students. They are so well trained that they can start working productively on day one.

According to this version of hiring practices, university graduates are longer term investments.

They need a lot of job training at the outset, but their broader university educations enable them to adapt to new situations when existing types of jobs become redundant and are eliminated by employers.

On the other hand, community college students in obsolete jobs have to start from scratch and go for another round of "employee training" schooling to learn how to do a new type of job.

In my dad's younger years, employers want to hire people who have enough schooling to be literate and to be competent in simple arithmetic and mathematics.

Employers of the time don't seem to require anyone with more complex abilities or knowledge for most jobs.

Although more recent generations of employers sometimes pay much higher salaries and provide much better working conditions to employees with more formal education, these employees are not otherwise valued due to their education alone.

When employer management personnel have less formal education or more education than the employeed, it can become a source of discomfort for management, creating negativity toward the employees.

When management and employees have about the same formal education, which is the commonplace during many of my dad's younger working years, the relationship is no better.

Simply doing the job efficiently is evidently more important in employment than developing or fully benefiting from the wider mental abilities of people doing the job.

However, formal education that helps people to question the fine points of the job can also be seen as an asset by some employers.

Formal education that helps people to think about ways of improving performance and the gross measures of productivity can be very useful to the employers.

But formal education that helps people to question the job itself is not viewed so favourably.

Formal education that helps people to reflect upon the employer's behaviour and goals in the wider context of societies and the employer's overall world impact is not always viewed positively.

More formal education of this variety can be threatening to authoritarian employers who see nothing beyond their financial profit ledgers.

Employers' ongoing preference for hiring people based on their ability and desire to submissively do "the job" relatively well goes under the misnomer of "work ethic".

A good work ethic would be much more comprehensive and include conscientiousness and enthusiasm for working well and making the work a positive force in the world.

The misnomer version of "work ethic" also seems to underpin the recurring generalized belief that the only good schooling is a "3Rs" (sic) education.

This belief continues to be very popular among some parents.

Ironically, however, the supporters of "3Rs" (sic) education seem to believe that the words arithmetic and writing start with the letter "r".

A religionist belief in "3Rs" is also related to the concept of "setting achievable goals".

In practical reality such goal setting seems to limit itself to what can be achieved with the least effort and within the most distant long term deadline.

In satirical terms, "I will complete grade one in elementary school before I am nine years old."

Or, in more serious terms, there is a consensus among leading scientists that there will be a tipping point in earth's human life support system within twelve years, so let's use a little less oil and hope that the scientists are wrong.

High hopes and great ambitions are only for "dreamers" who want to "change the world". Just think about paying your bills. If you save the world you'll be out of a job.

So if you don't save the world you will have a job?

It's better to just "be realistic" and "be satisfied" with a lifetime devoted to child-rearing and mortgage and motor vehicle payments?

Despite the extremely narrow focus and the extremely limited results that the "3Rs" (sic) and the "achievable goals" beliefs demands from education, it's not entirely surprising or unpredictable.

School systems themselves tend to reinforce the "3Rs" (sic) beliefs by producing post-secondary institution graduates who are:

a) functionally illiterate* or incompetent at communicating in their first language;

and,

b) unable to make simple calculations.

(* As early as 1987 The Toronto Globe & Mail newspaper reported that 25% of Canadian anglophone university graduates were then "functionally illiterate". In 2002, a young Quebec City CEGEP instructor I know complained about too many francophone students who were incompetent in their first language.)

Add to this literacy problem the inadequacies of audio-visual devices that should help teachers, such as computer software intended to detect and correct writing mistakes.

Commonly used "spell checks" (sic) appear to be the work of illiterate anglophone native speaker sorcerers with very limited knowledge of their own language.

The software "developers" apparently don't know the difference between "its" and it's". Whenever either word appears in a text document, the software says it's wrong.

This gives the impression that the software is not the product of a professional linguist devoted to accuracy.

The spelling check software is also flawed because it is based on nationalism.

This compromises and distorts language usage by depicting the location of the native speakers as the overriding and deciding factor in checking all "correct" spelling in all documents, no matter where they originate.

In short, nationalism rejects or ignores the universality of a language among native speakers in different nation-states where their language is the primary mother tongue of much of the population.

It's true that word usage does vary from place to place. A "collectivo" in one Spanish-speaking area is not the same thing as a "collectivo" in another.

In recent times, a "gringo" in San Juan, Argentina is defined as a farmer from Italy, not anyone from somewhere else.

But the spelling of "collectivo" and "gringo" are evidently universal in Spanish speaking communities. The same applies to many words in other languages.

There are exceptions in spelling in the English language, but all good dictionary versions of English spelling are correct.

However, this is unacceptable to computer spelling check software.

Instead of simply, automatically, and honestly accepting all correct standard variations in English spelling from all around the world, the spelling check software forces users to choose only one nation-state' version of the "correct" spelling.

Consequently, to be true to the realities of the English language, as well as French, Spanish, Portuguese, etc., a good writer must check every version of the language(s) of his/her document to determine whether a spelling "error" truly is a mistake.

The consequent necessity to switch from one nation-state version of spelling check software to another for many words challenged by the spelling check tends to slow down the editing process considerably.

Introducing nationalism to spelling check software also revives and reinforces an aspect of the nearly 500 years of the European national-colonial era (circa 1492-1948).

When presented with a list of choices among nationalist versions of the English language, a person using spelling check software to assist in writing is more likely to choose "English (United States)".

This choice is based entirely on an historic period during which a massive nuclear weapons arsenal and monetary wealth enabled the U.S. to have almost unchallenged domination over much of the world for more than half a century.

World power influences minds for generations.

Thus the U.K. game cricket remains very popular in Bharat, 70 years after the British Raj ends there. At the same time, Al Jazeera news in English is presented with U.K accents.

Equally notable, the frequent choice of "English (United States)" in spelling check software also reflects a strange but somehow widespread unspoken belief that English is not from England.

Restricting users to "correct" spelling defined by nationalism prevents users from benefiting from the rich variety of the entire English language.

Thus "colour", "theatre", "labour", "flavour", "centre", "neighbour", "tyre", etc. are always rejected as "errors" by the "English (United States)" software.

If the spelling is not U.S., it is automatically challenged as "wrong". It's literally, or limited literacy, saying "my way or the highway".

To top this off, if a writer chooses a non-U.S. spelling check, the software sometimes switches back to U.S. spelling in the midst or writing and/or editing.

Software based on nationalism can thus greatly narrow the educational choices available to students in schooling concentrating on computer-assisted learning.

The literacy produced by this schooling can thus also be inaccurately narrowed. So much for reading and writing.

Of course spelling check software confined by rigid nationalism is not entirely out of place in the "one-correct-answer-only" distortion of learning which dominates schooling for many generations.

Most recently, the inadequacies of schooling are further aggravated by a failure to teach young children how to read handwriting and how to write with a pen or pencil.

Abandoning this teaching for younger children is something entirely new.

It foretells that the generation(s) affected will require something the equivalent of a Rosetta Stone to understand thousands of years of human handwriting.

Given the diminishing attention spans caused by daily computer internet use, who will be capable of making the effort to use such a Rosetta Stone?

The school-inflicted inability of generations of people to know and understand the thousand years of written history immediately preceding their lives can be a huge handicap.

It accentuates the concept that not knowing and learning from the mistakes of the past dooms people to repeating them.

Total dependency on internet sources with careless unnoticed and uncorrected errors, gross subjectivity, chaotic contradictions, and deliberate disinformation is far worse than simply lacking the "usually reliable sources".

How many times a day are anglophones subjected to recorded news reports that always incorrectly substitute "there's" for "there are" and "less" for "few".

"There's many people here today, but less than yesterday." is a glaring mistake traditionally common among small children, not adult "news reporters" with much more formal education than children.

Putting the word "more" in front of words instead of using "er" after them renders listeners poorer linguistically instead of richer.

Internet sources are so obviously in extremely dire need of:

1) picayune, nit-picking, fastidious news editors devoted to good, clear, well-written communication of actual fact;

2) professional librarians responsible for assembling good collections of materials chosen for their excellence and accuracy;

and,

3) rigorous extensive research conducted by specialized meticulous scholars devoted to the pursuit of truth through honest objectivity.

In the past, such scholars have contributed to comprehensive encyclopedia articles offering information in great detail and a variety of interpretations of many historic events.

The rationale for the failure to teach students how to read and write the handwritten form is that computer keyboards make handwriting with a pen or pencil obsolete and archaic.

If that were true, everyone would have been writing entirely by typewriter and reading only typed script long ago.

Everyone with a university degree would only type because, during all her/his years of study, all paper submissions for professors must be typed, not hand written.

The keyboard is about a hundred years old, not a recent innovation. Yet generations of school children learn how to write with pen and paper during that century.

The standard typewriter keyboard in English is organized in exactly the same way as the standard computer keyboard in English.

Thus computer keyboards are very old tech.

The printing press is much older than the keyboard. More recent presses have used keyboards.

For a very long time, pamphleteers have made great us of very small printing presses.

Yet handwriting has survived both the printing press and typewriter technological innovations.

Schooling now wants to artificially change history by restricting people to only one means of reading and writing?

Computer writing fans and true believers also tell us that keyboard letters, numbers, and symbols are far superior to handwriting if the goals are "security" and "privacy" to help prevent fraud and other crimes.

This is at odds with prescriptions for medicine in doctors' handwriting. They are often so secure and private that pharmacists must call doctors to read the prescriptions.

At the same time, the computer software generally available is not capable of recording and reproducing a signature by duplicating or accurately simulating the intent and result of a person using a pen or paper.

This indicates that computers are not competent forgers capable of reflecting the fact that no two signatures are exactly the same, even if they are the signature of exactly the same person.

Each signature by the same person can reveal attention or inattention to detail, as well as happiness, sorrow, stress, fatigue, and other human emotions that are being felt by a person at the moment s/he is holding the pen.

Different versions of a person's signature do show common characteristics which indicate it is the handwriting of the same person. This is an additional challenge for all forgers.

A computer producing a signature cannot express such typical and distinctively human writing characteristic.

A computer producing a signature is incapable of creating a signature that can pass careful human inspection for forgery.

A computer producing a signature can only produce identical signatures which show only the characteristics of the software, screen, and/or printer.

These characteristics are simple machine features and variations which are common among many machines.

They are like the worn, damaged, and faulty keys of a typewriter or the varied keystrokes of different users of a typewriter keyboard.

Only the keystrokes of different users express personal attributes.

Signature forgery remains an art. Like many human arts, it remains beyond the capability of computers.
They lack talent and are not "gifted". They are incapable of human "genius".

Forgery of signatures requires a highly skilled and practiced human physical hand and a disciplined, artistic, and creative human mind, or a "soul", not a programme designed by an algorithm.

Software lags far behind in the human art of forging a multitude of very diverse handwritten signatures. Software capable of such a task might never be invented.

But when fewer people learn how to write with pen or pencil, who will be capable of distinguishing between real and artificial writing?

Mediocre software could then pass off some very poor imitations for authentic signatures. Nobody would know the difference.

Computer generated "signed" historic documents could be invented using poor forgery computer software to support or justify departures from actual historic documents.

Illiteracy, ignorance, and skill losses engendered by over-dependence on computer and internet technologies in schooling do not foretell better future outlooks for humanity.

Dropping handwriting in schooling also looks suspiciously like a marketing campaign by the computer and internet corporations to boost sales and the use of their products.

This can also simultaneously deny schooling to the lower income majority of humanity. They might be able to afford to buy pens or pencils, but not computers.

Like illiteracy in various times and places, computer ownership and paid internet access thus become social indicators for differentiating between the moneyed and unmoneyed.

People in the "poor" countries and neighbourhoods can all have cellular phones instead of potable water or nutritious meals.

But they can't afford the expensive most advanced versions of the technology.

Families have to pool their money to pay for the credits needed to get access to their electronic phone messages and "social media" accounts.

Single parents on minimum wage have to work extra hours to pay the big "smart" phone bills on top of the day care charges.

On the positive and challenging side however, the present state of affairs does promise a growing future for the field of adult education.

Of course it will require a great deal of hard work on the part of the adult learners to develop the hand muscles needed for handwriting.

Adult learners will also have to develop advanced self-correction skills to eliminate all the calcified errors implanted by the current schooling system.

Workshops about making sustainable economic lifestyle choices should also be in high demand, along with counselling help for electronic device dependency and addiction.

This will draw from data bases about impulsive and involuntary gambling addiction.

Long before all these problems and ramifications of present and future education times are upon us, my dad goes back to school by enrolling in the provincial government's correspondence course programme.

Remote learning is about pen, paper, and post office delivery, not satellite links or educational television stations.

Computers and internet are off in an unknown future.

My dad is in his entering his 40s at the time. His previous formal schooling is nearly twenty years earlier.

He can't be a full-time student at an educational institution.

He has to continue working during the daytime to pay for the mortgage, the car, and me, even though my mom also has a job.

Equal pay for equal work for women is still a very futuristic concept reserved to "odd" people who are not in government or the "main stream".

This is also an era before people in our province of residence can simply write a formal education equivalency examination to get credit for the informal education of their life's experiences and work.

My dad's situation is complicated because his schooling is in a different province and the provinces don't recognize each other's schooling as being equal.

One province will always claim that its schooling is better than the others and so deny credit to people schooled in another province.

Many years later, my partner Mariko and I find a similar disdain for "outside" degrees in the U.K., based on the European era superiority complex.

If a degree is not from a European university, it can't be equal. European degrees are "better".

This same type of provincialism rules in Canada's provinces when my dad decides to continue his formal education.

So he must prove himself to his province all over again.

Yet at least some Canadian universities seem to recognize the equality of formal education from different provinces when I complete my undergraduate degree.

They set no special conditions for admission for applicants with undergraduate degrees from a variety of other provinces.

At the time, at least, four-year degree from U.B.C. is recognized as an "Honours" degree by Ontario universities when I inquired the year of my graduation.

At U.B.C., all degrees in my faculty are four year degrees, at the time, and an "Honours" degree requires extra course work, not just four years of study.

When I apply to transfer my MSc studies from UofT to the U.S. UCLA however, that institution shows its U.S. superiority complex by requiring me to take extra courses.

I am accepted but decline the invitation because of the huge exorbitant rents charged in Los Angeles (U.S.A.). A year of studies there would wipe out all my savings of the time.

At least my dad's encounter with provincialism does not stop him. He studies diligently and presses on. The province sells him almost everything he needs.

With the exception of his oral French classes, all the course materials are mailed to him by parcel post.

He completes assignments and sends them in for marking. When he has to write exams, they have to be sent to someone with one of several acceptable occupations.

In my dad's case this means a corporate lawyer who works for the same employer as my dad.

The lawyer comes over with the exam, sits quietly and makes sure that my dad complies with the exam time limit.

Then the lawyer sends the exam directly to the government for marking.

Working and taking correspondence courses at the same time makes my dad's life very busy on top of his writing, gardening, little theatre acting, and socializing.

My dad only has time to take one course at a time, consecutively. In my full-time schooling as an adolescent, I can do all of every grade's courses in a single year.

It takes years of dedication and perseverance from my dad to try to complete his studies by taking only one course at a time.

So by the time I reach my mid-teens my dad is still taking secondary school correspondence courses. In some cases we're taking the same courses.

We have the same text books but he has to buy his, while I rent mine for a small fee.

We don't discuss course content and don't collaborate in our studies. In retrospect this seems like a missed opportunity for both of us.

When my dad studies recent history the text books are describing times he actually lives and understands just as well as the text book writers, if not better.

That's probably one of the reasons that he always gets better marks than I do, almost perfect scores in all his course work and exams.

My lack of experience and adolescence hold me back?

My dad seems to lose interest in the formal education system's correspondence courses when I start university. I don't know why.

By that time he is completing a French language course at night school.

He probably stops taking courses when comes to realize that by the time he can complete all the correspondence courses that the province demands he will be retired.

In a more advanced formal education system he would get credit for his life experience equivalency and we might be studying at university together.

My dad does continue his education through opportunities at work, taking advanced mathematics and other courses that aren't in the provincial curriculum.

(Finite Mathematics course at age 50)

He never loses interest in learning until the final years of his life.

The provincial correspondence course planners never seem to recognize my dad's desire to learn.

Their "required courses" outlook, based exclusively on processing adolescents through the schooling system for the first time, makes no concessions and gives no acknowledgement to the efforts of adult learners.

This rigidity of "correspondence courses" thus excludes them from the central concepts of adult education.

At the same time, unfortunately, for some years my dad's high marks and general progress in course completion do not get the credit they merit with his employer.

My dad's supervisor clandestinely makes sure that my dad does not benefit from his studies.

My dad's many applications for better posts with higher salaries are successful, but the supervisor vetoes attempts by other departments to transfer my dad to their staff.

Thus the supervisor effectively attempts to undermine my dad's adult education by making it seem all in vain.

The supervisor says that my dad is such a good and valuable worker that he is indispensable and so can't be given up to any other department.

Valuable doesn't translate into promotion or more income from the supervisor's department.

When my dad eventually discovers this interference he tells his supervisors that he will apply for every post he sees until he gets out of the supervisor's department.

Only then does my dad get to move on to a better position with an improved income.

The supervisor clearly puts his department ahead of my dad's competency, learning ability, and academic advancement.

The supervisor is effectively putting his personal and his department's interests ahead of the interest of the employer's need to make the best use of the staff available.

It is imposed "dead end" job planning.

My dad has a more interesting and educational encounter with another supervisor in a previous job.

My dad discovers that his supervisor is furthering his adult education by reading a book about the psychology of getting employees to do what supervisors want them to do.

So my dad continues his own adult education by reading exactly the same book and using it to teach his supervisor not to be so manipulative.

After reading the book, my dad does exactly the opposite of what it says the employeed will do when a supervisor tries to apply the book's theories.

The supervisor's intentions to turn my dad into an obedient trained animal are thwarted.

Adult education can be so egalitarian and liberating.

WHY ADULT EDUCATION
(my day and night studies)

My own journey into the field of adult education begins when I'm barely a legal adult. The age of majority is 18 and I am 21.

I have just completed a Bachelor's Degree and thus become only the third person in my family history to attend and graduate from a university up to that time. Others follow.

The previous two grads are from an older generation. One is my dad's brother and one is my mom's brother.

They each have a Bachelor's degree, one in engineering and one in history.

But I will become the first person in either family to go to graduate school. Only my cousin Steve follows me, to date.

Steve is the first and still only member of the family with a PhD.

My Bachelor's degree is in political science.

I choose this field for various reasons, including the poor chemistry and physics teachers I have during my final two years of secondary school.

I'm highly motivated to study science, but those two teachers do nothing positive to encourage that motivation.

Yet, in spite of their poor efforts and interest in helping me to learn, I finally do earn a Master's of Science degree.

Long before that accomplishment, I find my late teens and early twenties are an ideal time for studying political science.

It' a time when Canada suddenly becomes an exciting place to live for the first time in my life. I'm just beginning to comprehend that I'm not living in a European colony.

The Centennial Year, the Montréal Expo, and the arrival of Pierre Trudeau as justice minister and then prime minister are all bringing Canada to life after a hundred years of sleep.

This should not become the first time that I'm finding Canada so exciting. But the previous times are called "rebellions" and are quashed by colonial forces.

I'm many generations removed from those dramatic times.

Even my grandparents are too young to remember Louis Riel's "crazy" future vision of Canada as a bilingual, multicultural place.

My schooling makes only passing reference to him, dismissing him and glossing over his significant accomplishments.

He is written off as a "murderer" who executes an anglophone settler. In fact the "settler" is a rowdy criminal who tries to unsettle Riel and his compatriots.

Riel founded two of the ten provinces. He was denied his seat in Canada's parliament after being democratically elected by his constituents in fair and free elections.

Riel was also the only Father of Confederation to be executed. His co-Father lacked the foresight and courage to defy demagogic anglomaniacs and cancel the hanging.

All of the above is not textbook "knowledge". I have to reach these conclusions from non-schooling sources. This is part of my adult civics education.

In my earliest adult years, Pierre Trudeau quickly becomes a Canadian hero and is re-elected many times until he retires after about 16 years in office.

Only one prime minister remains in office longer, William Lyon Mackenzie King, the grandson of a leader of one of the quashed rebellions.

Pierre devotes his long stint as prime minister to "participatory democracy" and "a just society".

He strengthens human rights in Canada, including the language rights promised when the U.K. colonial era officially ended and during Riel's "rebellions".

Pierre Trudeau is the most positive, progressive, intelligent, inspiring, and stimulating prime minister of at least my lifetime, to date.

All of his successors, to date, have failed to do much more than keep the prime minister's seat warm in parliament. Most do very little.

One tries to turn back the clock and return Canada to an era long before Pierre and my adolescence. Another seems well-intentioned but lacking in all other respects.

When one of Pierre's sons becomes prime minister there is much nostalgia and hope, but there is no apparent interest in aggressively pursuing the "just society" agenda with the same vigour of Pierre.

Pierre annoyed some voters by honestly say that if they didn't like his policies "they can vote for somebody else".

His son seems too ready to discard policy to win re-election for his party.

During the election campaign before he becomes prime minister, Pierre's son declares that he will change the electoral system to reflect the actual votes of the electorate.

When the committee appoints to do the work produces divided opinions, Pierre's son folds and electoral reform disappears.

Imagine if Pierre Trudeau had done the same in his quest for human rights. It took Pierre 14 years of very hard work, negotiation, and compromise to get results.

His son gives up on electoral reform within only a couple of years of becoming prime minister. Pierre's son makes no memorable, inspiring speeches, unlike his father.

Pierre Trudeau delivers speeches that rally people to action and to the support of his policies.

Pierre inspires me in a way I have not experienced since listening to U.S. president John F. Kennedy during my childhood.

He's a champion of civil rights and the exploration of outer space. No one has come close to these advances in all the subsequent years of U.S. history.

The only exception is Barrack Obama and his advances in domestic health insurance and environmental protection in the U.S. His speeches show a great deal of intelligence.

Like Pierre, Barrack is a university law professor and political activist before taking the top political job.

When Pierre arrives in Canada's parliament, unlike the nearly three years of JFK's presidency, I'm old enough to participate in Canadian politics.

I'm no longer just a child in a very restricted formal schooling system with a life run entirely by the adults around me.

Ironically, after Pierre becomes prime minister, during my four years of studying political science at a Canadian university there is almost no mention of Canada.

The only courses available about Canada are extremely boring. One is about Canadian politics and government, but it lasts only half a semester, about three months.

This short course is taught by a younger Canadian professor who will later run for city council, and lose.

The other course about Canada is an evening class that I choose to take during the summer. It's my first experience of as an adult night school student.

It's a Canadian history course taught by an older Canadian professor who starts out by saying, "I know you are all here for the love of three credits."

Hearing these words my motivation to attend classes and study for the final exam is greatly diminished. I settle for a "pass" and the "three credits".

My attendance in this course is also hampered due to a secondary school student who does her best to sabotage my university year by toying with my emotions.

She lives in another town. I set aside my course work and give her advance notice that I'm coming to visit. She expects me.

But as soon as I arrive and call her to arrange to meet somewhere, she greets me by saying, "I'm washing my hair." So she can't see me. Maybe later.

Her words are said matter-of-factly and without even a mild hint of an apology. It's as if I'm a complete stranger who is arriving as an inconvenient and complete surprise.

When I drop her much later, after trying very hard to fit into her hair-washing schedule, I explain that it's because she treats me "like a rock", not a person.

This nasty game ends up having implications for my graduate studies too.

Accepting a "pass" mark in any course lowers my third and fourth year average, a factor in admitting or rejecting applicants for graduate school.

My high first and second year marks are given lower priority by the school of graduate studies when deciding who gets in and who does not.

Perhaps my "first class" results in my first two years are given some weight to counterbalance the "pass".

Trying to get around the "pass" problem and the lower morale it creates is not the reason I decide to study adult education.

It's the reason that I opt for a "diploma programme" instead of a Master's degree course of studies initially.

Fortunately, department politics, along with encouragement from the department head, help me to transfer into the Master's degree programme.

The department head seems genuinely puzzled and surprised when he says, "Why aren't you in the Master's course?"

His writing inspires me to go from political science into adult education. I view the two fields as the equivalent of science and applied science (engineering).

The first choice of many of my co-students in political science is to go into law. That's the preferred field of applied political science. This shift is encouraged.

The next step is to go into politics and run for office, or to start a lifelong career in the cushy permanent government bureaucracy that outlives elected representatives.

In Canada one leads to another. Career public servant Lester Pearson becomes prime minister.

When I'm in political science, a law background is valued in electoral politics because some students assume that people who study law can be orators capable of making speeches that can get them elected.

Another, perhaps better founded assumption is that politicians who study law are very valuable in the process of writing good laws.

They can challenge bureaucrats with law degrees and not get dissuaded because they don't understand how to write good laws and don't know how they can be applied.

It's certainly true for law professors Pierre Trudeau and Barrack Obama.

Now, however, the idea of elected law grads writing laws seems to be out of fashion among candidates and voters.

This may explain the existence of poorly-thought-out laws without adequate safeguards to protect the public from errors and abuse.

The latest non-lawyer government of Canada, just before Pierre's son, finds itself losing court cases because its laws are not well enough written.

I give passing consideration to studying law, and do take some great Vancouver People's Law School night courses for adult learners, taught by young practicing lawyers.

I take these courses over a period of years well beyond all of my formal education.

These truly adult night school courses are that good, exceptionally good. I never feel drowsy or have an urge to be somewhere else. These courses are free too!

Somehow I don't have a great enough interest in getting a law degree. So I look elsewhere for a field in graduate studies.

At one point I'm also considering taking a Master's degree in urban and regional planning as applied political science.

But I don't bother to apply because the department calendar seems to say that I lack some of the prerequisite undergraduate courses to qualify for acceptance.

Ten years later, when I finally am studying for a Master's in planning, I meet a former co-student in political science who is working for a provincial government planning department.

When I tell her why I didn't study planning ten years earlier she tells me that she also lacked the requisite courses but applied anyway. She was accepted by the department.

Never underestimate your qualifications.

As things turn out, the enthusiasm of the chief of the adult education diploma programme and the adult education department head help to swing the balance in their field's favour.

The chief and the head introduce me to some pre-course reading that's filled with references to adult education being crucial to improving societies and promoting democracy.

Thus adult education becomes the applied political science for me.

I'm moving from theory to practice, from studying politics and government to participating in improving the citizenry underpinning them.

My Master's degree studies at university turn out to be my longest continuous experience as an adult night school student.

The setting is also unique. All courses are held in the living room and dining room of the university president's house. The bedrooms contain only profs' office furniture.

The house is on a cliff side overlooking the ocean. There is a very large back lawn. The entrance driveway goes through a green garden.

It's a very pleasant and comfortable non-classroom setting that is especially appropriate for adult learners taking night courses. Faculty and students are de-institutionalized.

The faculty and students can use this very large house because the university president of the time prefers to stay in his own home instead of moving into official residence.

We are a less than a ten minute walk from the university library but feel remote from that campus centre due to our distinct building and its setting.

Our students also distinguish us from the rest of the university.

Recent graduates such as me are the least common type of student here.

Most of the students in my department come to the department directly from their workplaces instead of coming from the central campus area and studying here fresh out of undergraduate studies.

This is a unique experience for me. For the first time, most of my co-students are older than I am. Some are considerably older.

Many of the students have full-time day jobs.

They range from school teachers and community college instructors to employee trainers who tell me that they are taking courses here to qualify for promotions or pay raises.

At least one works for the Canadian government immigration department.

This means they can only take courses at night. So most classes are scheduled for after their work hours.

The working students seem to get off work a bit early to arrive at "the house" on time.

Almost all classes begin in late afternoon and last until early evening, with a short break along the way. This is earlier than night classes I know, which start and end later.

The only exception among classes is the diploma programme seminar, which is held just after lunch, once per week.

Some of the working students don't seem to appreciate the fact that adult education is not the same as child/adolescent schooling.

Some here probably do want to improve their work by learning something new that challenges what they "already know" and consider normal.

It never occurs to me that some of these people are the equivalent of the school teachers who had absolute power to rule over my academic life only a few years earlier.

We share exactly the same status now, in courses here.

The department head gives them no particular extra respect or consideration, regardless of their occupations and years of experience*.

Nor do I. I simply find them novel and somewhat old.

(*Experience can include calcified errors.)

The department head, Dr. Coolie Verner is an older person and veteran of the much quoted U.S. military adult education training programmes of wartime past.

Dr. Verner is also a former member of the U.S. military, who often happily says that he is now a Canadian citizen.

Happily misrepresents Dr. Verner.

He is a chain smoker nicotine addict with deeply etched lines framing a normally grim facial expression that startles onlookers when it breaks into a smile.

Taking his courses is hazardous to one's health during the years before smoke is banned from public places.

His experience and expertise in adult education are clear and at times I perhaps overly respect him for them. His words about adult education and democracy impress me.

He tolerates my rare teasing, when for instance, during a class exercise I bellow out "Times up!" in a gruff voice mimicking his manner of ending small group discussions.

Other students caution me about mocking Dr. Verner, saying my imitation is too close to reality.

Calling younger professors by their first names is commonplace, but few of us dare to call our department head "Coolie" to his face or in private.

An older school principal among the students does so one day and gets a very cold, negative yet unspoken reaction. Dr. Verner recoils physically as if gravely insulted.

The principal quickly he reverts to "Dr. Verner".

Dr. Verner shows some disdain for teachers from the child/adolescent school system who don't seem to recognize the great differences between their work and adult education.

So my qualms about the schooling system fit in well with Dr. Verner's apparent attitude.

However, Dr. Verner is not unfriendly. He invites a community college teacher to his home for what the teacher calls a very strong alcoholic drink.

When Dr. Verner invites me to his home too I decline because I'm not going to accept an alcoholic drink from anyone.

Dr. Verner tells many tales about his years of field work in adult education and his encounters with colleagues who want "certification" for adult educators just like school teachers.

He disagrees with them and argues well. A good adult educator, as many profs in the field say, needs broad life experience.

That requires much more effort than taking courses to get a certificate and going through a practicum to have the certificate validated.

Adult educators need to be good students who must learn as much as they can about every adult learner they encounter. There is no such thing as a "typical" adult learner.

If an adult educator is not willing to learn about and from his/her students, s/he is at a great disadvantage and more likely to fail as an educator.

Dr. Verner talks about an adult student who he helps to apply for a job. The applicant is successful, but worries about not being able to actually do the job.

So, after the hiring, Dr. Verner helps the student acquire the skills needed to do the job. This means that Dr. Verner also has to learn new skills.

This reminds me of one of my partner Mariko's co-students at l'Université Laval who studies to become a French teacher in a school system.

After graduation, a school board hires this student to teach Spanish, not French.

So she has to learn Spanish while she is teaching it. In the process, she also has to make sure that she is always one textbook chapter ahead of her students.

This is applying adult education to a specific and immediate need -- keeping a job instead of getting fired.

Dr. Verner also tells us about arriving in a backwoods U.S. town with a group of adult educators. They sit in the town square talking together and playing a guitar.

Some townsfolk approach and ask why the group is in the square. The adult educators reply, "We're here to change things."

The townsfolk say, "We don't want to change." So Dr. Verner and his colleagues leave town.

I am conscious of this story during my later adult education efforts in Saskatoon and Dyingtown.

Dr. Verner's funniest story, which none of us get, is about going to a conference.

While talking about adult education for all, a member of the assembled asks him why there is any point in providing educational opportunities for "ditch diggers".

Dr. Verner replies that it gives the digger something to think about while holding a shovel.

Dr. Verner repeats this story in every class he teaches and I am in all of them.

My personal favourite among his stories is the one about his undercover work as a night school student.

He says he sometimes enrols in night school classes to check out the state of the field.

When asked to introduce himself, he pretends that he's a "longshoreman", someone who unloads cargo containers at a seaport.

His rough appearance and gruff manner and voice make this impersonation credible.

At least that's what those of us who never actually meet someone in this type of job believe.

I get some sense of what Dr. Verner might feel like in a night school class when I'm taking some degree courses a few years later.

I find myself critiquing the poor quality of some of the classes run by some of the profs.

One of the profs who I criticize most severely actually agrees with me, calling the approach of his university academic department a "consensus of mediocrity".

In contrast, some years later I take a non-credit Spanish refresher course and compliment the instructor for teaching me some new things about language teaching.

Every adult education experience is an opportunity to learn something unexpected.

During part of my time in the adult education department I'm involved in Prime Minister Pierre Trudeau's first and almost failed re-election campaign.

But I never miss classes or fall behind.

I take the campaign to class by screening a political party training film for door-to-door vote canvassing. We use it for a group discussion.

It is a professionally made film starring John Candy and other Canadian comedians.

Learning from this film for my own door-to-door canvassing work is also part of my experience as an adult learner.

I am responsible for organizing all of the student residence building polling divisions on campus for Pierre's re-election campaign.

My official title is chair of the constituency first-time voters committee. I never work as a political organizer before this campaign. I'm learning how to lead people.

My very enthusiastic and hard-working team of multi-province volunteers and I manage to win the most votes in all but one division by 80-90% margins with heavy voter turnout.

The division we barely win is composed entirely of people studying to work in churches. We do only token campaigning there so as not to disturb their meditations.

We seem to be the only winning team in the constituency. The candidate is not re-elected in the total riding vote count.

I also bring the election campaign to class by inviting a junior cabinet minister to come to speak at the department.

The house living room is overflowing with students sitting in multiple rows of chairs.

Elections are great adult education learning opportunities.

In the comprehensive exam that I write as part of my graduate work for my M.Ed., I incorrectly predict that civics education will be the prime focus of adult education in future, rather than job training.

I'm imagining a future world in which employment is finally obsolete and people govern their lives themselves instead of by proxy or by relinquishing power to employers.

The election campaign contributes to delaying my Master's graduation by about a year while I postpone choosing a political thesis topic.

My first choice is to study the work of political cadres in Chuang Hwa as an area of adult education. I find reading about their existence fascinating as an undergraduate.

Unfortunately, as my second year political science seminar leader (later Rt. Hon.) Kim Campbell tells us at that time, her thesis on the People's Republic of China is difficult because there are so few materials available in English.

Three years later I find myself in a similar situation. So I abandon the cadre research with a sigh and look for an alternate topic.

My delay in graduating is minor compared with some PhD students in my department, who get extensions to finish theirs for one reason or another, including work demands.

I understand that some of them are in their tenth year of trying to complete their degrees. I enjoy the department, but I don't want such a lengthy delay.

During my delay I have three journeys related to my field of study and final major research paper.

I go to Montréal once and Ottawa twice.

One of the PhD students organizes a government-paid trip to Montréal to meet with local adult educators and to attend a conference.

This adds to my personal adult education and introduces me to people and French terminology I don't know.

I seem to be the only one in our group who knows French. So while a francophone speaks English to the group he asks me the English equivalent of "troisième age".

I mistakenly blurt out "third age", not yet knowing that the correct equivalent is senior citizens.

I'm also overconfident about my knowledge of the Métro and cause the group to arrive late for an appointment on Côte des neiges.

When we return to our university another student and I are responsible for translating some of the printed matter we are given during our trip. I think we get most of it right.

So the Montréal trip furthers my adult language education.

My two journeys to Ottawa are about partisan politics and my final research paper.

I'm an alternate delegate to the national policy convention of Pierre's political party. I also attend a local policy conference in Vancouver.

At these events I also further my adult education by taking part in various types of meetings wherein delegates and alternates discuss policies and make recommendations.

My more directly academic-related visit to Ottawa is to study the federal government's official languages training programme.

I show up at the Carson Road facility devoted to this programme practically unannounced. I am warmly received and assigned a desk in the instructors' office.

I report to the office every workday for a month and talk to office mates, the language instructors, every day. They give me piles of material to either read or copy and take.

They encourage me to take the French language skills test given to federal employees, so that I can better understand how that experience feels.

My French skills get a 3.5 rating out of 4 on the test. I'm happy but I think the test is overestimating my skills of the time.

I have to wait until my journeys with a Carioca French teacher to feel that my skills are closer to 4. That will be my first personal private language tutor adult education.

The focus of my final M.Ed. paper becomes political thanks to the language teachers and my access to government department libraries.

Teachers give me articles from <u>Le Devoir</u> newspaper which reveal the contents of a leaked report criticizing the government language training programme.

I later stumble upon the actual report in another department's library in downtown Ottawa. I start reading it and taking notes there.

However, when I ask the library staff to make a photocopy of the whole report, they tell me that it is not a public document and I should not be reading it.

This stimulates my curiosity and annoys me so much that I write to the minister responsible for the report, explaining that I have already read and taken notes from the report.

I say that I have the impression the government is opposed to academic research. The minister sends me a copy of the entire report.

My month in Ottawa and subsequent reading of all the materials I receive there persuades me to write a paper with similar conclusions to the leaked report I manage to get.

I conclude that the year language training begins, the federal government is reacting to the <u>Royal Commission on Bilingualism and Biculturalism</u>.

Essentially, it says Canada is unaware that it is in the middle of a crisis because the founding principles of anglophone-francophone equality have not been respected. So the federal government goes into crisis mode and grasps at the best known language training programmes available in Canada, e.g. Voix et Images de France.

It will take years before professional language teachers are able to counter this knee-jerk, make-shift approach by developing language programmes made specifically to fill the public and public servant needs involved in providing public services in both official languages.

This process is underway when I meet the teachers and they give me samples of the materials they are creating for their public employee students.

In the first years of government language training, the French course materials are using the ones that I have in secondary school.

These materials were devoted to activities far removed from the work of public employees in Canada, such as buying baguettes in Montmartre, Paris.

Thus my adult education and academic efforts are advanced by my trips to Montréal and Ottawa during my first graduate studies.

I will later live in Ottawa for a year while taking a one year honours degree for post-graduates at what is then one of only two journalism schools at universities in Canada.

For me this too is an area of applied political science.

Along with my cross-Canada journeys and reflections about a thesis topic, a bus ride across my then province of residence also delays my graduation.

The bus is part of a pre-internet mobile continuing education project for people working in remote rural hospitals.

It takes four years to finally get this project off the ground by the time I start my Master's studies.

Due to my studies of satellite communications, I think the project is outmoded.

Why not just provide remote hospitals with access to satellites?

I am also not impressed with the planning of this project. There are too many groups involved who don't seem interested in having a successful outcome.

The bus itself is the worst example. It's a forty year old vehicle that is being refurbished and refitted with shelves and audio/video equipment and materials.

The bus houses a specialized mobile library.

When it rolls into town, local health specialists can use their time between work shifts to listen to and view audio/video recordings aboard.

The age of the bus and the difficulties that engenders with upkeep and maintenance almost cripple the project.

The bus has ongoing mechanical problems, halts in the middle of a busy highway, and creates a situation leading to a car accident.

After that, there is swifter work to make the bus work well.

This is my first experience with an adult education project that lacks adequate pre-thinking, planning, and dedication to success.

It's just a school project that is supposed to contribute to the prestigious reputation of the university health sciences departments.

In the end, it makes no such contribution, although the bureaucracy responsible probably stamps it as a great success.

I write a detailed memo to the body in charge of the project, severely chastising them for contributing to a traffic accident by not giving enough care and attention to the project bus.

I attend a meeting of the body and do not recant or soften my stand.

In response, instead of admitting shortcomings and cooperating to improve their work on the project, the body denies all wrongdoing.

The person chairing the body declares that since the people in the body are devoted to health sciences they would never do anything to endanger anyone's health.

What mechanical problems? What car accident?

I resign from the project in protest.

I have one student colleague in this project. He's also annoyed and tells a member of the body that he should "take lessons on how to buy a bus".

But my colleague is very worried about my memo. He also decides to apologize to the member he criticized.

This student later begins working at the body's university health science centre.

Somehow the bus project continues to run and silently disappears over time. Satellites are on the horizon and the internet will not be far behind.

Of course I do benefit from my part in this project. It's part of my education as an adult learner.

My personal gains include the opportunity to visit some very small towns that I only glimpsed in passing in years past.

I meet some of the locals and find them welcoming and generous. In one slightly larger town I'm able to visit some cousins. I enjoy the scenery too.

On top of this I receive a graduate student assistance fee which is more than ten times the usual scholarship funds I earn to pay for my first years of university studies.

Adult education brings expected and unexpected benefits.

I also learn about how people running organizations approach problem-solving during a crisis that they don't want to acknowledge or attempt to honestly resolve.

Reality can be dangerous for people who want to portray themselves as all-knowing professional experts instead of humble adult learners.

No matter what I do, I'm always in political science?

As alluded to previously, while describing my trips to Montréal and Ottawa, between adult education and community planning I study and work in another field of applied political science – community journalism.

I approach this field with a preference for local media where I can be a writer who knows his readers and their lives personally.

Weekly community journalism is close up and personal. It is connected to small communities. Everyone is a source. Everyone is a story.

We are neighbours who can see each other every day.

Community journalists get constant feedback that is not anonymous and which is helpful in improving the basic tasks of reporting the news.

Daily mass media does not attract me because it centres on famous but anonymous writers with anonymous readers.

Daily mass media journalists are writing to a remote, unknown audience. Strangers are writing for strangers.

Readers only know the writer as a byline and maybe a photo. Writers know almost none of the readers.

Knowing people makes it easier to communicate with them. Not knowing people makes communication vague and open to widely different interpretations and decoding.

Daily mass media columnists have to come up with an instant opinion-of-the-day on whatever is reported in the news at the moment.

Who has a thoughtful opinion on anything and everything every day, on demand and to deadline?

A columnist for a weekly community newspaper can talk to and get to know a large percentage of his/her readers personally.

With this personal knowledge and understanding of her/her readers, the columnist can come up with clear and comprehensible writing that his/her readers can more easily relate to.

It's much like being an adult educator in a small group of adult learners. Both the educator and learners can learn from each other.

My particular approach in community media is to highlight and emphasize the opinions of my readers, so long as they are not local politicians or other opinion leaders.

I want to give people who are never heard an opportunity to be heard. I also want to encourage them to think carefully and express themselves clearly.

I stand on sidewalks and knock on people's doors to ask them what they think.

As a newcomer and outsider in town, I am poorly informed and unaware of what people are thinking. So I tread lightly.

I ask positive questions and request suggestions for making local improvements. I don't ask about "big", "general world issues". I keep the topics very local and thus learn.

My first two questions are: "What do you like about this town?" and "What would you do to improve it?" The suggestions are positive and interesting. I learn a lot.

In so doing I don't encounter people with political or ideological agendas who want to push negative, prejudiced, or extreme views.

Instead they just say what's on their mind about local things that they can see and know firsthand.

Trying to get to know readers personally can also have a downside.

When I interview some younger women who are depicted as "sunshine girls" in a summer season newspaper photo item, one of them agrees that the portrayal is sexist.

All the other women just shrug off the experience and make no mention of sexism. So the person I quote on sexism stands out.

After that, she stops smiling and saying, "Hi!" to me when we pass in the street. She just rushes past me, pretending I'm not there.

By coincidence, before she appears in the paper and I interview her, I hope to become one of her friends. That hope vanishes.

Community journalism is personal and it's taken personally.

Overlapping my later studies in community planning, I write a different column explaining the "District Plan" for the local region and ask for comments from locals about the contents.

I get to know the planner hired for the job and later meet him by chance, in passing, when I'm at planning school. We're surprised to see each other again.

A few moments later, one of my profs tells me that the planner says the locals give him "a hard time" when he's working on the plan in the area where I write.

Good! I'm glad that I motivate participatory democracy in my work as an applied political science worker.

Isolated and aloof professional planners in all fields please take note. This is part of your adult education.

I won't meet any planners who truly understand their need for adult education until I meet Carlos Nelson at IBAM* and Lícia do Prado Valladares at IUPERJ** in Rio de Janeiro.

(*Instituto Brasileiro de Administracão Municipal)
(**Instituto Universitário de Pesquisas do Rio de Janeiro)

They are "third world" planners sharing my great interest in favelas. They are the only planners I meet who are completely devoted to putting democracy first in planning.

Ironically, a nasty military dictatorship is ruling over them during most of their lives before we meet.

At this time, dictators are finally withdrawing and gradually letting a fully democratic system of government return to Brasil.

We talk together in their offices for hours. It's an immense pleasure and a wonderful adult education opportunity for me.

I first see Lícia when she is publicly chastised and rebuked by a local politician at a public education meeting held at IBAM in Rio.

Planners sorely need to have this type of severely critical encounter.

Carlos and Lícia are both delightfully and enthusiastically aware that planners need to work very hard to learn from the people who actually live in human communities.

Planners need to make sure that the lead role in the planning process belongs to the people, just as it is in planning adult education programmes.

The people, the adult learners are the ones who end up living with planning results and mistakes.

When the project work is "done", the architects and urban planners can just disappear and move along to their next paid projects.

They take along pretty pictures to show only the clever and artistic sides of their work, not the consequences for people who have to live with it.

Ultimate client leadership can help to reduce the planners' mistakes because they have the deciding say in planning their homes, their neighbourhoods, and their communities.

This is an adult education experience for both planners and their ultimate clients.

We are all equal participants in our own ways and we all have something to learn and contribute.

Another one of my adult education experiences involves a "business communications" course held in a fancy hotel in San Francisco (California).

That's when I'm working in a mining company office, so it's an all-expenses-paid trip.
It seems to be a good course and I learn a great deal.

Unfortunately, the company person sending me on the course, after taking it himself first, disagrees with everything I learn and try to put into practice.

This is my weirdest experience as an adult learner. Sending me on the course is no more than a tax deduction business expense for the mining company?

Titling this section of <u>An Adult Book About Education</u> "Why Adult Education" is more than a double entendre.

"RADICAL" INTERLUDE

Between community journalism and planning I spend sixteen months writing for what turns out to be the propaganda department of a "clean" coal company.

I'm supposed to be editing a monthly "employee" newspaper, but it's only a four page corporate flyer composed of dull information and drab photos.

The department head calls it "prosaic" writing. Prose? The content is limited to pictures of groups getting work safety awards, trucks, reclamation work, etc.

I'm supposed to be the "community relations assistant" so I try to take my title literally and assist the community to balance off my very restricted "journalism" work.

By happy coincidence one of the profs and a finally graduated (?) doctoral students from my adult education studies are working in a relatively nearby town.

I contact them and they come to visit. They suggest that I get in touch with the local community college representative in the mining town where I live.

I go to see him and take along some ideas for community development. The pages I type for him include quotes from famous Canadian adult educators such as J. Roby Kidd.

Kidd is the author of How Adults Learn. Five years before I meet the college rep, Kidd establishes International Council for Adult Education (ICAE) in Toronto.

So Kidd should be well-known by the college rep.

Apparently not.

Consequently, instead of a meeting of colleagues devoted to furthering adult education, the college rep turns my appointment with him into an awkward moment.

I don't know anything about the rep's background or interest in adult education, but his reaction to Ruby Kidd tells me that I'm not talking to an adult educator.

The community college rep opens our meeting by slowly reading aloud my quote from Roby Kidd as if it were evidence in a case against Kidd.

In a cautious and concerned tone reminiscent of Cold War witch hunts, the rep dismisses Kidd saying "That sounds radical."

Perhaps in fear of being associated with a "radical" Kidd, the rep ignores my offer to cooperate with the community college to further adult education in the town where we both live.

Roby Kidd is an apparently insurmountable road block to adult education. My only hope is that the rep gets replaced. But I don't try to facilitate that desirable outcome.

I don't pursue the rep's comment about Roby Kidd with my two former colleagues from the adult education department.

When I mention the rep meeting with someone I know in a university "extension" department, he laughs and says that trying to work with both the mining company and the college sounds like a conflict of interest.

But it was worth a try.

ESCURO

During my first stay in the city, Córdoba, Argentina is a campus town with many choices for evening continuing education such as free lectures and courses.

My Carioca friend and I go to some free public lectures in the evenings.

Unfortunately, the El Monserrat, Instituto Goethe, and public library lectures use archaic, classical teaching techniques.

The most and least memorable is a short series of lectures on philosophy and linguistics.

A professor arrives with a pile of pages, reads them - head down - and then perhaps makes a token request for questions.

People who are still awake and interested are usually too anxious to leave after sitting quietly and listening only - for an hour.

If anyone does want the lecturer's monologue to continue, and so asks a question, the lecturer replies by merely turning back pages and rereading them, again head down.

He speaks of "universal" philosophical concepts, but refers only to Plato and other Europeans, ignoring completely Confucian, Arab, and other ancient Asian philosophy.

My friend and I agree that questioning this lacking would only appear insolent to local professors who believe that they are teaching anything beyond patience and endurance.

They are unwittingly giving all present a lesson in how not to further education.

In the end, all of us in the passive, drowsy audience do get something out of the lecture. A certificate baring our name is given to each of us.

Never before have so few done so little to get so little?

This is one academic document that I stow away in a file folder, out of sight.

COURSE INTRODUCTIONS

Adult education can last a lifetime, after skipping the first 15 to 20 years of life, depending on the cultures and societies surrounding the adult.

Unlike what we learn at the beginning of our lives from our parents, extended families, earliest friends and experiences, and from institutions such as primary and secondary schools, adult education can only start when we become adults.

At that time of life, no matter how hard we may try to remain the same and prevent all changes in our lives, something is going to happen to alter our life experiences and cause us to learn.

In spite of our belief in the myths of stability and routine, adult learning is unavoidable and happens in spite of any imposed restrictions on the adult, even if the restrictions are self-imposed.

This makes adult education the only part of lifelong learning that is available to anyone living anywhere, regardless of apparent constraints such as those imposed entirely due to a person's income, geographic location, religionisms, visible sexual characteristics, etc.

In this sense adult education and adult learning are truly and naturally egalitarian and democratic.

The unpredictable and unexpected random events of everyday life will always and inevitably predestine every one of us to learn something.

This goes far beyond the sudden natural emergencies of earthquakes, storms, flooding, and other predictable and recurring natural events that are somehow always surprising and shocking us.

Life itself is a learning opportunity that is unavoidable.

No matter who we befriend and become long-term partners with, we cannot avoid learning something from each of them.

No matter how carefully we prepare for the next steps in our lives, by thoughtful planning, asking our elders questions, or undertaking scientific research, we will find ourselves learning more than we are ready to expect.

Learning is often almost invisible and always surprising.

Impossible tasks and apparently insurmountable obstacles can almost magically vanish before our eyes because we somehow learn how to deal with them.

Even if we fail to deal with them we still end up learning something, if only about ourselves.

Learning from our failures can lead the way to our later successes or at least help us improve our ability to cope better with failures.

Even if we don't learn how to swim we can wear bathing suits. We can still enjoy crossing the sea in boats and visiting natural underwater aquariums too.

Although most of the remaining pages of this writing are largely and apparently about attempting to plan adult education within the confines of schooling institutions, the story nonetheless continues to be about adult learning itself.

The remaining pages of <u>An Adult Book About Education</u> could be described as a story about learning how not to plan and how to plan adult education and learning.

Experience, expertise, and good intentions, and lack thereof, appear to be the main obstacles to planning adult education and learning. But there are no absolute barriers.

COUSIN JIM'S COURSE

My cousin James Douglas starts his adult life and education in the Canadian Armed Forces. His life is indelibly marked by this experience in at least two ways.

He talks of his "misspent youth" and reveals, with reluctance and embarrassment, a beautiful, colourful, big tattoo of a mermaid covering one of his arms.

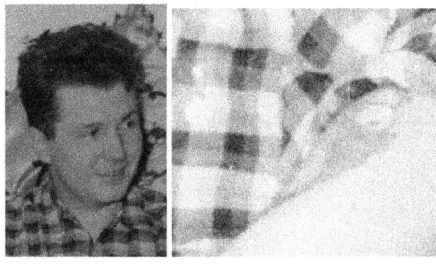

The less evident highlight of his youthful learning is that the military takes him to Japan.

After I explore Japan for a few years and return to Canada with my partner Mariko, Jim takes me aside to talk about the most profound thing he learns in Japan.

It's love.

He meets a Japanese woman who he calls "the one", his true love. He shows me on a map where she lives at that time. It's somewhere in the southwest corner of Honshu.

Even as an older adult he still laments the fact that they cannot be together only because the prejudices of a world war are still festering in the decade after it ends.

In Japan, Jim learns that he can fall in love with the daughter of a former military enemy. He never sees her again but loves her for the rest of his life.

He marries Joy from New Zealand and has three children. He later marries Dianne from Canada.

He also works for a federal and a provincial crown corporation before finding something he prefers to do.

He becomes a sculptor and teaches sculpting to adults in a school board night school. His course is very popular and is well-publicized by a local newspaper.

It's not a class coming from his employment experiences.

People want to learn the skill that Jim is teaching.

My experiences with attempting to offer night school courses suggest that this is a very fortunate coincidence, not an inevitable, predictable outcome.

FIRST ATTEMPT

"City Affairs News"

I first try to offer a night school class for adult learners in Vancouver. The school board accepts my course idea and supports it right up to the first night of classes.

In retrospect, I wonder why I try to offer the course and why I get institutional support for it.

My course is related to journalism, politics, and local government.

Long before I know about Dr. Noam Chomsky's research on how much coverage different news media dedicate to certain stories and not others, my course is going along the same lines.

Chomsky is interested in international events, but my concentration is on municipal government and politics alone.

I choose that area because that government is closest to the people it serves but has the lowest voter turnout during elections where I am living at the time.

And my course is timely due to the upcoming municipal elections.

Federal and provincial governments are more remote and distant from the people they serve, but on election days these governments get about triple the number of voters.

I think that the big differences in voter turnout are at least partly because the news media pays much more attention to provincial and federal politics than to municipal politics and government.

So my adult night school class is supposed to try to find out if that might be true.

Instead of planning a course, I could just do the research myself. But I'm a victim of my own education.

Perhaps I'm copying what I learn from university professors in graduate school. They get their students to do at least some of their research for them.

Unlike the profs, my intention is not to publish an academic work with my name on the cover and a smaller print acknowledgement page inside that's giving my students a general thank you.

I simply want to find out if the news media is paying very little attention to municipal politics and government, aside from a weekly summary of the city council meeting highlights.

I create a course explanation for students. It reads:

The average person gets so much news thrown at him/her every day that it's increasingly difficult to take it all in.

Radio, television, and newspapers just keep spewing out news, without knowing whether anyone is really listening or reading.

In this course we are going to listen and read. We are going to make a note of what we hear and read in the news, one time each week, and then meet together to talk about what we have heard and read.

We won't be talking about all the news, because that would take far too long, and our efforts would have to be enormous.

So we are just going to listen to, and read news about what's going on inside the city limits of Vancouver.

By concentrating on Vancouver, we will be able to be very aware of what's news in Vancouver, and to compare radio, television, and newspapers very carefully.

What we are doing is comparing what radio, television, and newspaper editors think is worth telling us about Vancouver.

Also, we are finding out how different editors present this news. Then we can criticize editors' choices and presentations.

<u>At Home</u> we will be listening to, or reading one news report each week, and keeping a very short diary about what we hear or read.

<u>In Class</u> we will be comparing notes about our findings.

I also create work sheets for students to fill out.

All they have to do is read a newspaper, watch a television newscast, or listen to a radio news broadcast one day each week and take a few notes.

I imagine that they are already following the news and that's part of what motivates them to take my course.

The students' notes in the work sheets will first report whether or not there is any municipal politics and government news.

Then the students will report the subject of the news and how much space, (lines or minutes), the news media devote to the municipal politics and government news.

In class, each student will report what s/he finds out and we'll talk about it as a group.

That's the basic idea of the course.

Here is a sample of the structure of the diary sheets that I prepare for each student.

Brief description of each Vancouver story	Position of story in the newscast	Length of story (in seconds)	(evening news, or late night local news)
1. _____	1st, 2nd or 3rd story heard ___, or later ___.	1 - 15 ___, 16 - 60, or 60 or more ___.	
2. _____	1st, 2nd, or 3rd story heard ___, or later ___.	1 - 15 ___, 16 - 60 ___, or 60 or more ___.	
3. _____	1st, 2nd, or 3rd story heard ___, or later ___.	1 - 15 ___, 16 - 60 ___, or 60 or more ___.	
4. _____	(this story, and any more, are later.)	1 - 15 ___, 16 - 60 ___, or 60 or more ___.	
5. _____		1 - 15 ___, 16 - 60 ___, or 60 or more ___.	(IF MORE, USE OTHER SIDE)
6. _____		1 - 15 ___, 16 - 60 ___, or 60 or more ___.	
7. _____		1 - 15 ___, 16 - 60 ___, or 60 or more ___.	

Vancouver News Watched Wednesday September 22, during _____, on Television Station ___.

I also create a media habits questionnaire, a self-test, and a personal questionnaire for the first night of classes.

first night

Your Media Habits

(Please check the answers which describe your habits.)

1. I watch local TV news: (i) once in a while ___
                          (ii) nearly every day ___
                          (iii) almost never ___
2. I listen to radio news: (i) once in a while ___
                           (ii) nearly every day ___
                           (iii) almost never ___
3. I read a Vancouver daily paper: (i) once in a while ___
                                   (ii) nearly every day ___
                                   (iii) almost never ___
4. I read a Vancouver weekly paper: (i) once in a while ___
                                    (ii) nearly every week ___
                                    (iii) almost never ___
5. I almost always watch the same TV station for local news.
   yes ___, no ___
6. I almost always listen to the same radio station news.
   yes ___, no ___
7. I almost always read the same Vancouver daily paper.
   yes ___, no ___
8. I watch local TV news most often on: ( ) CBUT Channel 2 ___,
   CHAN Channel 8 ___, CKVU Channel 21 ___, KVOS Channel 12 ___
9. I have Cablevision. yes ___, no ___
10. I watch Vancouver Scene on Cable Channel 10. yes ___, no ___
11. Usually I hear radio news on: CKNW ___, CJOR ___, CKLG ___,
    CHQM ___, CKLG ___, CFUN ___, CJVB ___, CJU (CBC) ___,
    KARI (Birch Bay) ___, CFRO-FM (Vancouver Coop) ___.
12. Usually I read: The Sun ___, The Province ___, The Courier ___
13. Local news is covered: well ___, poorly ___, average ___
    Comments? (use other side) _____

first night

Your Self-Test On Some
Vancouver City Affairs
                        name _____

1. What do you think are the two most important news
   stories about Vancouver so far this year?
   (i) _____ Why? _____
   (ii) _____ Why? _____
2. Name three people who are now members of Vancouver City
   Council: (i) _____, (ii) _____,
   and (iii) _____.
3. How many people are now members of Vancouver City Council?
   _____
4. Does Vancouver have a ward system? yes ___, no ___
5. When does Vancouver City Council have its regular
   meeting? _____
6. Name some of the candidates for Mayor of Vancouver
   this year: _____
7. How many people are elected to the Vancouver Parks
   Board? _____
8. How many people are elected to the Vancouver School
   Board? _____
9. What's the date of this year's Vancouver City election?
   _____

```
                                                       first night

           Personal Questionnaire

       (Please don't write your name on this piece of paper.
       The reason we'd like you to fill out this questionnaire
       is so we'll have a better idea of what kinds of people
       are interested in this kind of course, and why.)

       1. How did you find out about this course? _____
       _____
       2. Why did you decide to take this course? _____
       _____
       3. Have you ever worked for a TV station, radio station,
          or newspaper? yes ___, no ___
       4. Have you ever been involved in city politics anywhere?
          yes ___, no ___
       5. Have you ever belonged to any sort of Vancouver
          community club? yes ___, no ___
       6. Are you new in town? yes ___, no ___
       7. Do you live in this neighbourhood? yes ___, no ___
       8. If not, what area do you live in? _____
       9. Are you: working at home ___    going to school ___
                   working somewhere else ___  retired ___
       10. Are you: single ___, married ___, other ___
       11. How long did you go to school? elementary ___
                                          high school ___
                                          beyond high school ___
       12. About how old are you? teens ___, 20s ___, 30s ___,
                                  40s ___, 50 or over ___
       13. male ___, female ___
       14. Is your family income: high ___, average ___, low ___.
```

To help students, I will bring along samples of stories to note in diaries from newspapers and do a practice exercise with past news stories.

I record a CBC Radio local news broadcast and CBC sends me a transcript of it.

I'm well prepared. Now all I need is students.

To attract potential students, I approach the news media for free publicity. I send out news releases about my course, one for newspapers and one for radio and TV.

All releases are identical in content for each newspaper, except for the first and last paragraphs.

There I use the name of the newspaper that will receive the release and the media type.

Here's the content of my newspaper news release, with the name of one of the newspapers getting it.

> Headline: Highland Echo to be Text Book
> For New Night Course

You might find yourself reading The Highland Echo more carefully, if you enrol in a new night school course starting at Britannia Centre on Monday...

Local papers, radio, and TV are the course textbooks.

Anyone who enrols in City Affairs News, the course, should get a closer look at Vancouver city affairs, and how city affairs news is reported by the media.

"We're going to read and listen to the news like everybody else, But we're also going to take notes," according to instructor and community journalist Don Anderson.

"We're going to find out what different media people think is news in Vancouver, and what news they think is most important."

> "And we'll see what happens to news stories when different media – radio, TV, papers – get a hold of news."
>
> City Affairs News could make reading the news a whole new experience.

The Grandview edition of <u>The Highland Echo</u> community newspaper publishes my entire news release, omitting only paragraph three.

<u>The Voice</u> programme brochure at Britannia Community Service Centre mentions my course briefly too.

I script a shorter version for radio stations. Here is the content with the name of one of the radio stations, a rock and roll station targeting a teen audience:

> Did you know that C-FUN is going to be a textbook? Vancouver Night School will make C-FUN News required listening for five weeks. It's for a new course called City Affairs News. It's about Vancouver. It's also about the way different media report Vancouver news. City Affairs News begins September..., at Britannia School. Register early to avoid disappointment. Phone the Vancouver School Board and ask for night school information. The number to call is ...

I send this one to eight radio stations, including one where someone from my secondary school works, Wayne Cox at CKNW. Wayne does not reply.

I send an item to Vancouver Co-op Radio. They read it on a Thursday night at 7:30 p.m. I introduce my item by quoting the radio station's information pamphlet -

> "People in the community have an integral role
> to play in the development of news"

Here is my item to Co-op Radio:

> Most people in the community might have to be made more aware of the alternatives in news services, before playing a more active role in news development.
>
> A new night course called City Affairs News could be a model of how to build public awareness of news service alternatives.
>
> People in City Affairs News will look at Vancouver's many news services. The course begins Monday.... The course lasts five Mondays.
>
> Phone the school board to find out how to register. The number to call is...

Vancouver Cooperative Radio will be a textbook for City Affairs News. Other local radio news, TV news, and newspapers will also be textbooks for the course.

City Affairs News is both a public affairs course and a journalism-for-the-layperson course. It's about Vancouver. And it's about the way different media report Vancouver news.

The most enthusiastic response I get from commercial broadcasters, and the only interview, comes from C-FUN, which has a public affairs broadcast.

Sunny Lewis, the broadcast host records an interview with me at the station and airs it soon afterwards. I listen to and like the results.

As usual, the school board publishes its six page newspaper advertisement showing the multitude of night school courses it's offering.

The first half page of this advertisement alone lists 103 courses. Each course on every page is described very briefly in the same style small font.

A person wanting to take any particular course has to go through a lot of looking, and perhaps squinting, even if s/he knows in advance exactly which course or type of course s/he wants to take.

Courses are listed under the names of the educational institution building where they are held.

In <u>The Vancouver Sun</u>, the six page advertisement is on pages 51 to 56 in one edition. My course is at the bottom right hand corner of page 55. In another edition my course is in the same spot on page 39 of 35 to 40.

In this morass of identical type I try to attract attention to my course be writing something more controversial.

So if anyone has the patience and time to get to the second-to-last page of the advertisement, bottom right hand corner, they might notice my course.

I write: Heard the news? Believe it? What are the papers, radio, and TV really telling us about what's going on in Vancouver? Test the local news services, and yourself. Enrol today, in City Affairs News.

The fee listed for the five week, two hour per session course, is $9 per participant. That's about $1.11 per session per person. (Today it would probably be $9/class.)

Some courses charge more. Some charge less.

Other courses about communications media, one similar to mine, are also listed in this multi-page advertising.

I notice that someone is offering a course similar to mine across town.

It's a class about general news coverage. It's more critical of news and news media in general, involving more analysis of the news media.

It's run by someone named Angus who is teaching at a community college on the opposite side of town from Britannia School.

I call the instructor, posing as a student, to find out about his media and adult teaching background. He tells me that he writes items for the dailies and has taught adults.

I write to him afterwards, apologizing for posing as a student and asking about collaboration between our classes.

I say that it's unfortunate that the school board does not put us in touch so that we can work together.

He phones to say that he's not offended and thinks my type of call is "standard procedure".

He also offers to send his students to me if his class does not get enough people to hold the course.

Before classes are scheduled to begin, the school board asks me for an oral blurb, something to use to answer questions about my course when potential students call for information.

Apparently the number of phone calls the school board receives is substantial. So my course is set to go ahead as scheduled.

Later on I wonder if the blurb I write for people calling in to ask about my course makes them lose interest.

Instead of explaining my course the same way as I describe it during the radio interview, I try to write abrupt one-liners to lure in students, just as I do in the six page newspaper advertisement.

My blurb should be a simple but attractive course description.

My one-liner blurb is simply meant to say that the relatively small amount of attention given to municipal politics and government by the local news media means that a person has to pay close attention to what little news coverage is available to find out what's really going on.

A factor about my blurb that's beyond my control is the way people say and hear it. They aren't talking directly to me or asking me questions. I'm not the one replying.

So the tone and voice of the people at the school board who are reading my blurb out loud will strongly influence the blurb's message. Are they monotone or enthusiastic?

When I arrive at Britannia for the first evening of adult night classes I meet only two people.

One wants to take the course. He seems to think that my course is going to be about uncovering secrets.

At this moment I know that my course, as planned, cannot function with only one student. I wonder what I can do to help this person learn something.

The other person I meet this night resolves this situation for me. He works for the school board. He very apologetically says my course is cancelled.

He says it isn't cancelled earlier because of the large number of phone calls asking for information about my course.

So all the good, careful planning I do to prepare for this course and all my publicity efforts are for nought. No matter how good the idea, a course needs participants to make it happen.

The City Affairs News course is only a learning experience for me. Perhaps if all those callers interested in my course had talked directly to me instead of the school board?

SECOND ATTEMPT

"My Biography"

This adult education project doesn't start out or end up being what I plan.

It's a unique effort that no one before or since attempts to do anywhere in the world that I'm aware of, to date.

Perhaps it all starts in a museum on an island in Malaysia, five years earlier.

There I'm bored by displays which seem to be entirely made up of the decaying fancy old clothes of some long dead elite.

Later I realize that almost all of the autobiographies and biographies in the public libraries are also only about the moneyed and famous.

The exceptions I read are about the long walks of Harry A. Franck who crosses South America, Japan, etc. If he is elite for his non-moneyed extended adventures, so am I.

Autobiographies or biographies about the vast majority of people living throughout history are extremely rare or non-existent.

It's as if most lives are of no importance and make no contributions whatsoever to humanity. It sounds like an employer's version of history.

For employers, lives are no more than "human resources" to be extracted and exploited. After they are used, i.e. employed, the remains are discarded.

We know the names of people who own companies but not the names of generations of their employeed.

If a person is not moneyed or famous, her/his life is of no consequence. S/he has no place in human memory or history.

So I attempt to offer an autobiography and biography service to anyone and everyone who is not moneyed or famous.

I offer this service on a cost plus basis, instead of trying to make a lot of money at the expense of the vast unknown unmoneyed and not famous majority.

I see almost limitless potential for this service and conclude that it will be something I merely start and others will continue due to the huge volume of work that will be involved.

This service will ultimately change the way that the lives of most people are recorded, remembered, and immortalized, creating a much more comprehensive and balanced picture of human history than an elites-only version of events.

The non-elite will be just as appreciated and vulnerable to critique as the elites.

I'm assuming there is a great need for this service and it will be widely sought after. People can be very sentimental about their elders when they get older.

A few months later, after attempting to make this service known in the small city of Saskatoon, I am puzzled by the reactions.

My first encounter is with an older person who works at a supermarket and wants to give me some tips about marketing.

But he is not very interested in my actual project or in encouraging me to pursue it. It's just a product for him that can be sold.

Much more puzzling are the reactions I get from a certain group of local people.

Somehow the people aware of and involved in tracing family ancestry, i.e. genealogy, are convinced that the words autobiography and biography mean exactly the same as genealogy.

They confuse the dead with the living? They don't understand that I intend to interview the living only? There will be no medium or clairvoyant in the room.

Due to the very perplexing and incomprehensible misunderstanding, every time that I try to make my service known, I always get the same response: "Somebody is already doing that."

But nobody is - not in this town.

Aside from the apparent lack of comprehension, semantic problem, or stark illiteracy, the main message I'm getting is that if somebody is already doing something, nobody else should or can do it.

So alternatives and competition are bad? This is coming from a "capitalist" society. What about fresh perspectives and collaboration?

Forget about aspiring to become a doctor or a musician, or anything else because there are already doctors and musicians and other people are already doing the things you want to do?

So there is only one musician and one doctor living in Saskatoon? This must make entertainment and medical treatment very difficult for locals.

No wonder the very large, brand new hospital in Saskatoon at the time seems to be largely an empty building.

I also don't see any advertising for local talent concerts during my months in town.

The jazz festival that my partner Mariko and I attend must be entirely performances by out-of-town musicians.

In this type of one-person-per-field world view, we all have to wait until the people already doing something either retire, die, or leave town permanently.

Meanwhile the rest of us can only do what we don't want to do? What a bleak future. What a sad outlook on life.

The irony is that absolutely nobody in this town is doing what I'm planning to do.

The only slight advantage I have is that I know two people. One I am just meeting and another is someone who studies with me at university.

The one I know is the PhD student who organizes the Montréal trip when I'm in the adult education department.

But my former co-student only wants to talk about department politics at his workplace and his plans to change employers.

He invites me to lunch at the employee cafeteria near his office.

On the way back, he introduces me to a colleague specializing in "global education" by saying that I'm "living it".

The person I'm meeting for the first time in this town is the son of a friend of my parents.

He's friendly and seems to be supportive of my project in Saskatoon. But he too doesn't understand it.

He says I can pay $50 and get full access to the local university genealogical archives.

A more helpful person is Susan at the public library. She is local but she does her university studies in Montréal. She throws me a bone.

She hires me for a one time stint as book discussion leader for a regular meeting of the library reading club.

The book she chooses for me is about a gringo's experience in Nippon.

With Mariko's help and suggestions I turn this into a session about intercultural encounters and "the water trade"*. (*The ebb and flow of bar districts in Nippon.)

I do some research and, thanks to Mariko, learn much about Kabukicho along the way. It's an ancient entertainment district of Tokyo.

I learn so much because I tell Susan about a book describing Kabukicho. She quickly gets it for me through inter-library loan.

This is a bright moment in Saskatoon.

So is meeting the writer-in-residence Betsy Warland, who says good things about my writing and makes suggestions to help me to publish it.

Susan invites me to her home too, for a meal with some local writers. They meet regularly but this is the first I hear of them. It's very late in my stay in Saskatoon.

This city and its province are experiencing an aging and declining population at the time of my stay.

Does this explain why so many of my new-found acquaintances expect everyone to die before I can start interviewing anyone?

Thus I would be involved in genealogy?

I make one more attempt to clarify my project.

I try to go around the apparent misunderstandings and intransigence by introducing my project through a night school course. I propose it to the local school board.

In the course I will explain my idea and train people how to put together autobiographies and biographies of the unmoneyed and not famous locals.

But the school board rejects my proposal outright, stopping me dead in my tracks.

The board says that my autobiography and biography writing course is a genealogy course and somebody else is already offering that course.

No amount of careful explaining can persuade the local schooling elite, or most other people I encounter in Saskatoon, that an autobiography and a biography are not equivalent to or the definitions of the word genealogy.

It's baffling.

A semantic mistake in a town and at a school board prevents an adult education course that would help enable most people to be recognized as having lived and contributed something to humanity.

Nobody among the local elite is willing to try to learn that there is a difference between the words autobiography, biography, and genealogy.

How does the school board's reluctance or refusal to try to learn fit in with promoting the goals of adult education?

My efforts to gently persuade, not argue, are all for nought.

There is no motivation to learn here?

Only my own personal adult education is advanced. I learn more about ignorance.

THIRD ATTEMPT

Multiple courses

In a place that I call Dyingtown, my partner Mariko and I try to offer several courses that are sure to interest many people.

We go to a community college instead of a municipal school board.

The college administrator is very enthusiastic and very helpful.

While we promote our courses through the local weekly newspaper, he makes specific mention of our courses there too.

In this very small town, our courses should be widely known and stirring up at least some curiosity and maybe interest.

The college administrator also invites us to his "service club" luncheon. The club asks Mariko to prepare a presentation about our work and courses.

Everything is going in our favour. For the first time we can be sure that we'll be able to teach adult learners through a Canadian educational institution.

Our courses and workshops include oral French and Japanese language classes; a Japanese culture class and briefing; a class about being a good visitor anywhere on vacation; and workshops about creating and teaching adult night school classes based on personal interests and knowledge.

At the administrator's suggestion, we propose some of our courses at the local arts centre too.

The coordinator there is also very enthusiastic and helpful. She's relatively new in town and relates to us very well. She is helpful in other ways too and invites us to events.

Despite the variety of courses we come up with, the final results are not much better than anywhere I try to offer courses in the past.

Almost every course, briefing, and workshop that we propose at the community college and arts centre is cancelled due to lack of interest.

We do end up teaching some students, despite all the cancellations. Three people who want to study French come to our apartment.

Unfortunately, we feel that we can only charge the fee advertised by the community college.

Since the college is not paying us the difference between the fee and our income, we're only receiving about a dollar an hour for our work.

The students can easily figure this out, but none of them offers to pay anything more than the advertised fee. They have no qualms about using us as slave labour teachers.

These students have regular jobs and good incomes. They can afford to pay much more than 33¢ each an hour for the class they enjoy so much.

On the final night of classes, our students don't hesitate to tell us that they know our course is a great bargain and well worth their regular attendance.

Every one of our student comes to every class and remains for the entire class. There are no absences or drop-outs. No one disappears.

But nobody asks us if s/he can continue to study with us as a group or privately, either now or in future. No one wants to pay a fee that would even pay for our groceries?

Again, our students have time to spare, regular jobs, and good incomes. They are a substitute teacher, a farmer, and a hospital cook.

They could easily continue to study with us and pay the regular tuition instead of 33¢ an hour.

After the final night of classes, we never see or hear from any of them again.

Shame on them. They could at least be friendly and invite us over for a free meal. Maybe we could teach for food.

In Dyingtown, we thus do some virtually pro bono type work. We seem to come to Canada to lose money doing charitable work.

I prefer doing that type of work in the "third" world where I can help more people and at least make enough to pay my living costs.

Yet the often modest, minimum wage for teaching adults that we can earn in the "third" world is higher than our total income in Dyingtown.

In Dyingtown, we're ready and willing to offer courses through local organizations but they don't know how to make use of our skills.

Local people with our skills, experience, and training always leave tiny places like Dyingtown.

The people they leave behind might fill the vacuum but they might also object to our intrusion and find it threatening to their unchallenged local elite status.

These are some of the reasons that there are so many dying towns in Canada. The other reason is Canada's ageing, declining population.

Our willingness to live here and to offer our services is so unbelievable that even if they wanted to, the elite by default left behind here can't really cope with us or use us to their maximum benefit.

So they don't. They miss an opportunity.

The default elite left in charge of such small places have fewer qualifications, less experience, and less formal education than we do.

All the more reason that they could try to benefit from our presence and exploit us as a community resource.

Instead they find dealing with us particularly difficult.

Maybe we are a threat? Some may worry that we're here to take their jobs and become their bosses.

If they knew us they would know we have no interest whatsoever in replacing or ruling over them.

We're just here to see what it's like to live here and to offer our services while during our temporary, short-term stay. That threatens no one.

But the local elite by default don't know us and they don't try to get to know us.

Instead, they try to divert, deflect, discourage, and dissuade us so that we will just go away and leave them in peace.

Their relief and gain in seeing us leave town prematurely is at the expense of their community.

Young locals who are also locked out of the default elite's domain will follow us along the path out of town instead of renewing and strengthening their town.

The remaining sections of <u>An Adult Book About Education</u> will cover some conclusions, implications, and suggested remedies based on my encounters with night school.

NIGHT SCHOOLING IN THE DARK WITH RESTRICTED VISION

The adult education problems that Mariko and I observe in little Dyingtown are all too commonplace, regardless of population size.

The problems go well beyond a frightened default local elite and the overall handicap of not understanding the basic differences between teaching children and adolescents versus facilitating adult learning.

By force of habit alone, the schooling system itself is unlikely to fully appreciate the fact that offering adult education programmes is very different from administering schooling.

Adult education is more than a mere extracurricular activity to be run after regular school hours. Adult education is not a school club or sports team.

Yet, in too many places for too many years, adult night school is treated as if it were just such a side-line.

It appears to be an after school pot luck dinner or an evening smorgasbord with a menu that's almost haphazardly thrown together as an afterthought.

This misses an essential difference between offering adult education versus administering schooling.

Unlike regular daytime school classes, adult education isn't compulsory schooling. There are no laws forcing adults to go to school, unlike children and adolescents.

All adult courses are completely optional for all comers, like many activities and choices in life.

Financing is also different. All of the operating costs of day schooling are paid for out of education budgets that governments routinely pass each year.

Unlike the resulting, publicly-funded elementary and secondary schooling, adult education in night school is not tuition free.

It is not paid for with tax money in annual education budgets.

Adult learners in night school are often subsidizing the extended janitorial services, increased costs of light and water, as well as the extra wear and tear on the buildings, etc.

Thus, excluding the costs of building and maintaining schooling buildings paid for by government, adult education has to be as self-financing as possible.

This is why adult courses are only held if there are enough adult learners signing up to study, i.e. to pay the bills.

Unlike day schooling, night school has to justify its existence and cover all the after school hours costs.

Night school has to pay night school teachers. Their incomes are dependent upon collecting the fees paid by adult learners.

A minimum number of learners must enrol or there will be insufficient funds to pay the night school teachers.

When there are not enough adult learners, classes are cancelled and adult educators receive no income.

The adult educators experience in night school is thus very different from the experience of child-adolescent school teachers.

They receive a steady, year-round income with benefits, all guaranteed by the schooling system and the teacher's union contract. Education budgets pay teachers' salaries.

The only essential and unavoidable spending in night school is thus building services and maintenance, not the work of adult educators.

In effect, cancelling night school courses and thus not paying some instructors is an effective economy measure. It cuts the cost of the "staff" item in the budget.

Fewer classes mean fewer adult educators to pay.

So why expend any energy and funds to provide a great variety and number of courses for adult learners?

Night school can more pragmatically minimize its costs by offering only secondary school completion courses and employee training classes

One way or another, government and corporations help pay the costs of holding those "essential" courses.

Night school will prove its worth in great statistics showing unquestionable success, justifying public and private sector investment.

All night school courses provided will have 100% enrolment.

Night school will demonstrate that it performs a "valuable public service" by increasing the number of people with more formal education papers and by improving workplace productivity through employee training.

There is thus no need to try hard to attract adult learners for other types of courses, ones that don't get the government and corporate support that help to cover the costs of night school.

Understandably and clearly, schooling employees who run night school are also the product of their day jobs.

They aren't running night school because of their devotion, commitment, or dedication to adult learners and the field of adult education.

They are simply helping adults complete the curriculum they dropped out of in youth; or, assisting employees or potential employees to gain and keep jobs.

These are minimal and "achievable goal" versions of running night school.

Night school run out of a strong dedication or commitment to adult education would require administrators to work much harder to fill most, if not all of the night school courses available.

This would produce far more than high school diplomas and job skills. Adult learners would be enriched in far more senses and far more profoundly.

Their societies would be too.

In the process, the abilities and experience of adult educators would not be lost or squandered by cancelling courses.

Adult education would be more highly and widely valued, appreciated, and supported.

Unfortunately, for generations, the whole idea of comprehensive and extensive adult education programmes in night school remains a low or non-existent priority.

More night school for more adult learners is evidently an area of little or no interest to schooling institutions.

Night school is a largely unexplored territory that is treated as if it were of marginal importance to many school teachers and schooling institutions.

And it actually is marginal to them, in a sense that at least parallels the L.B.E. (Language Business Establishments) and other corporations which dabble in adult education primarily for money alone.

If L.B.E. do help adults gain and improve language skills, it is only a haphazardly planned and often amazing side-line by-product attributable largely to the adult learners' efforts.

Night school is also dabbling in adult education in a very limited way.

The "regular" schooling system running night school is not intended or designed for educating adult learners.

"Regular" schooling adherents, proponents, and providers are fixated entirely and almost exclusively on childhood and adolescent schooling.

In this religionism, only "future generations" can make the world a better place.

Meanwhile, the adults currently in charge of running the world are a lost cause and must be suffered?

They are doomed to just muddle through unassisted by lifelong learning?

The only exceptions seem to be adult classes about babies. Expectant parents can attend many classes about preparing for birth and taking care of babies' needs.

But the same can't be said for raising children and helping adolescents to cope. Adult education could help parents while the babies are growing up.

Who has the time and energy to take such courses? There is maternity leave for mothers, and in some jurisdictions paternity leave for fathers too, but no parental leave for the post-baby years.

Parent training courses for adults trying to raise children and adolescents aren't even a side-line covered by night school.

Much broader adult responsibilities fare no better. One essential service has no adult training course to help applicants for the job.

No one can enrol in an adult education programme designed to train candidates or potential candidates for the work of political office in a democratic elections system.

No night school courses are offered to help novice politicians learn how to become effective and competent if and when they become elected representatives.

Political parties may have candidate training and briefing materials, but these are primarily about winning elections, not about governing well.

Elected representatives thus become dependent upon the experience, intelligence, benevolence, commitment to democracy, morality, and management expertise of veteran politicians, hired office staff, and lifelong government employees.

This weakens democratic processes by putting power and authority into the hands of popular and/or anonymous people who may only have more experience in not knowing how to govern well.

Hired office staff and bureaucrats with no mandate to rule or make decisions can become a proxy and parallel unelected government.

They may feel no need to make democracy their central goal unless they are truly zealous about it.

While thus ruling in a democratic vacuum, these office people may find that they have more in common with well-informed, expert, professional lobbyists than the untrained amateurs elected to be the official leaders of government.

The office people have no motivation to make democracy their central goal unless they are truly zealous about it.

Thus we can only hope that the adults now running the world won't do irreparable damage before the children are old enough to inherit the mess and to get their chance to try to fix it with equally little knowledge of how to do it.

Schooling institutions and teachers might help "tomorrow" but they leave today's world unattended by devoting themselves almost entirely to very closed schooling systems and plans.

Unfortunately, universities are not completely immune to the concepts of closed systems.

Some senior faculty members reveal this problem to me at one university.

They say that the graduate school chiefs of my years on that campus are opposed to part-time study programmes. I am in part-time studies at that moment.

I go to class and the libraries between work shifts.

Part-time programmes thus enable working people to get more advanced degrees.

How can one remain elite and rule the world if the masses have easier access to the same formal education and can gain the same qualifications and competence as the elites?

Voters thus excluded from equality by being denied access to adult education become adversaries of the elite and will rebel against the megalomaniac elites with superiority complexes.

This contributes to the election of destructive and ignorant anti-elite demagogues, nationalists, and right-wing populists devoted to excluding the offending elites from influence and power.

The world political, trade, and economic systems fall, Amazonia's jungle burns, and the human life-support system collapses.

Excluding people from access to the power of adult education has dire consequences which even the elites cannot escape.

It must be difficult for people with vested interests to develop unconventional, inclusive perspectives, even at a university where there are many different lecturers and millions of volumes of knowledge in the libraries.

Night school is different from university part-time studies in the sense that the campus seminar rooms and other flexible facilities lend themselves to adult education.

In contrast, as things stand, the schooling system's enabling infrastructure mitigates against adult education and a progressive, open, and activist approach to it.

This infrastructure is a product of schoolings' closed system.

Most school teachers and schooling institutions operate almost exclusively in the realm of highly standardized, structured, graded, and restricted child, adolescent, and even some post-secondary education, having fixed "curriculum", a compulsory limited number of texts, and a very restricted system of evaluation.

This realm of schooling is an almost hermetically sealed, closed system. It's absolutely confined, operating only inside the walls of institutional buildings.

All of the teachers working inside that architecture comprise a special cadre of the full-time, lifelong employeed.

They are certified professional teaching staff or, in the case of universities, tenured faculty members.

With this particular type of job security, teaching staff could almost do as they please. Unfortunately, the path of least resistance can also prevail.

Old habits are hard to break.

It can seem easier and more efficient to exercise maximum control over learners and to dust off the old, reliable lecture notes, as I find in Córdoba, Argentina.

Some students I know at one Canadian university tell me that they see their prof blowing the dust off his tattered pile of lecture notes at the beginning of the first class.

Trapped in the confines of their previous experiences, most school teachers and institutions are likely to have difficulty coping with, functioning in, and adapting to the far more open, freewheeling, precarious, and variable world of adult education.

Adult educators are better prepared for this world because they have no certification, tenure, or even basic job security in night school.

So they have to be daring, inventive, and outreaching toward adult learners.

Again, unlike the closed schooling system, most adult education does not have a captive audience due to laws or qualification requirements.

In closed schooling, pupils and students must be present for most classes because the legal system requires their physical presence.

If children and adolescents skip too many classes, the legal system can fine or imprison the parents.

Many older adolescents and younger adults who are beyond the age where they are legally obliged to attend schools, feel compelled to remain confined to closed schooling to avoid spending their lives in the worst jobs available.

In great contrast, most adult courses are absolutely voluntary. So they must attract, not coerce, pressure, or feed on the worries of participants.

Unlike closed schooling, adult education has to seem interesting and useful to gain participants.

Adult education has to be worthwhile, well done, and worth paying for directly, instead of indirectly through obligatory income taxes.

As currently conceived, good adult course planning must try to account for every conceivable interest of every conceivable adult.

It's also a scattergun approach to planning.

Quantity takes precedence over quality? We have to fill the two page night school ad?

Why bother?

The poor calibre of advertising and promotion itself* is likely to obscure and conceal rather than reveal that the choice of courses offered to adults is much broader than the "curriculum" imposed on pupils and students.

(*More about this aspect of night school later.)

To make matters worse, seasonal night school courses for adults are often planned as if they were completely superfluous to and disconnected from everything else in life.

The approach can sometimes appear to be much like movie makers trying to develop "blockbuster" films by casually reviewing scripts on their desks and saying "What if…?"

The movie could turn out to be very roughly based on whatever script the movie makers glance at because it happens to be on top of the pile.

Just like the pile of scripts, a night school course might be offered only because a stranger walks into a schooling institution and says, "I'll give a course on ….."

Mariko and I do just that. We are the embodiment of "What if…?"

As I learn in Saskatoon, an instructor and course can be accepted or rejected equally casually, without thorough understanding or consideration.

The ability, experience, and training of the "instructor" don't seem to matter to anyone. Adult course instructors can be anyone.

My cousin Jim and I are thus equal in the eyes of the Vancouver area school boards. But that's not true. I know nothing about sculpting.

Dyingtown's publicly-funded college never asks Mariko or me for our résumés or references. They apparently don't matter. Our courses are "non-essential"?

Just to clarify -

So long as there is no universal professional certification of adult educators, the ranks of professional adult educators will be dominated by people with graduate degrees in adult education.

Whether this is desirable or not is a matter of debate within the field of adult education.

However, night school teachers with degrees in adult education seem to be rare in my night school experience.

The same applies to L.B.E. (Language Business Establishments) staff hired as "language teachers", in that they don't have degrees in modern languages, language training, linguistics, or adult education.

However, in adult night school classes, teachers who are not professional adult educators with degrees in adult education can still be good choices, if they're capable of teaching adults well, in a well-organized, effective, and professional way.

Adult education supports the notion that adults can learn. This means that an adult can learn to become an adult educator.

But regardless of the educational setting or teaching, learning ultimately is the responsibility of the learner. We learners must study hard on our own.

In this sense we are all self-educated.

At the same time, the buildings, rooms, and maintenance staff requirements and costs of night school continue to get the highest priority and first consideration in planning night schooling.

All the courses and learners must be fit into institutional structures and furniture that are designed and manufactured specifically and only for smaller, growing people.

Elementary school desks and toilet fixtures are tiny.

Using daytime schooling buildings is only meant to reduce the costs of night school while perhaps increasing revenue for day schooling?

Or is it about providing supplementary incomes for some school board employees who teach "curriculum" to adults at night?

All courses and learners need to fit more than the economically viable, almost self-financing criteria mentioned earlier.

All courses and learners must also be fit into the routines and demands of scheduling afternoon maintenance workers for night shifts.

The top priority is carefully analyzing the building, room, and maintenance requirements of night schooling, not the adult education courses or instructors?

Adult education is required to "fit in". Schooling structures and maintenance predetermine everything?

This distorts the whole concept of adult education and catering to the adult learners' particular needs.

It's apparent that trying to impose a rigid, closed system on adult education is inappropriate.

Reversing this situation would no doubt help to improve the schooling system and contribute to its success rate.

Organizing and scheduling adult courses themselves seems to be almost an ad-hoc, secondary, theoretical, abstract consideration in night school.

It seems to assume that all adult learners always work exactly the same shifts, are full-time employees, and are only available for learning at night on weeknights.

Adult courses in schooling institutions are being planned and promoted as if they had to be entirely at the convenience of the schooling system, not adult learners.

It is as if adult education were merely an extension of closed schooling. Thus adult classes are offered by what some institutions call the "extension department".

Closed schooling norms also apply and take precedence.

In that system, since regular day students have absolutely no say in what subjects they're forced to study, why would adult learners be invited to participate in the planning of their own night courses beforehand or to change the plans while the course is in progress?

How chaotic and hard to control! Sure, for the "regular" schooling system.

But adult learner participation in pre-planning and changing courses in progress is a standard feature of adult education.

Without this participation, organizers of adult courses who are ruled by the isolated perspective and restricted experience of closed schooling are not adequately prepared or fully competent to create adult courses.

They need to solicit the help of adult learners before offering a course.

They need to know exactly who is coming to learn, why, and how the learners need to be approached, etc.

Adults are far more complicated than children and adolescents with free room, board, and funding who are cared for by loving parents at home every day.

Night school organizers are also adults, but they don't recognize that they need to get to know adult learners and how to adapt to help them learn.

A background in regular schooling does not give night school organizers the training and experience required to understand the adult learners' specific needs.

Thus people working in the isolated and restricted system of closed schooling can accomplish very little beyond almost guaranteeing that most adults will rarely, if ever, participate in many of the adult courses offered at the institution.

Adult learners will forfeit their class fees and drop out before completing a course because it doesn't fulfill their needs and becomes an unpleasant, tediously boring experience that is "a waste of time".

Participants will enrol in and return to the same courses only if they feel very comfortable about renewing their contact with the closed schooling system that dominates most of their youth.

This may be a similar feeling to the one of a prison inmate who becomes a repeat offender soon after being released because s/he wants to return to his/her familiar life behind bars.

Similarly, teachers who work exclusively in closed schooling probably feel most comfortable in that system. So they try to impose it on adult night school.

Applying the closed system model requires no adapting to the real needs of adult learners.

They can be treated as a passive audience of strangers needing to be controlled, instead of known, active participants in learning needing to be heard.

Using the closed schooling approach to adult education, the work of night school teachers can be done with minimal effort, innovation, originality, and/or imagination.

Night school teachers can merely repeat exactly what is done routinely in "regular" schooling classrooms filled only with children and adolescents.

This does nothing to improve the impressions that potential adult learners have of night school.

Some adults consider night school nothing more than something to do to pass the time when all other avenues of human activity and contact are exhausted or when life is becoming totally boring and there is too much spare time to fill with their real interests.

Adult education becomes a desperate escape route instead of something attractive, valuable, interesting, and worth doing.

Simply thinking about signing up for a night school, especially one held in a regular school building, is liable to bring back good and bad memories about:

1) going through childhood;

2) many years of compulsory schooling;

3) teaching and teachers of mixed quality, temperament, and professionalism;

4) challenges of adolescence;

5) pleasant and unpleasant people met along the way;

and

6) other learning experiences in life.

Those memories can rekindle mixed feelings about the past and prevent many people from wanting to voluntarily go back to school.

Since the same schooling system is running night school, it seems highly probable that the night school experience will not improve the way that adults already feel about school.

If they have their own children who are in the schooling system, the parents' perceptions of that experience could also be an influential factor in deciding whether or not to go to night school.

Notable exceptions as well as apparent financial successes are the employment-centred adult courses mentioned earlier.

But they're not truly optional adult courses. Employers require their employeed to participate for advancement and higher incomes.

This is a unique area of adult education in which coercion, pressure, and fear are involved in course planning and participation.

These adult courses are little more than the outsourcing of company training programmes to save businesses the costs of setting up and maintaining permanent in-house training departments and hiring a staff of full-time trainers.

But since these courses are tailor-made for employers' needs, these courses can also be somewhat more open than an extension of the closed schooling system.

My partner Mariko and I find this to be the case in the study programmes we design, manage, and run at private corporations.

Corporations just give us a general idea of what they want.

They leave the specifics to us to save the time and money needed to determine the actual, detailed employee training needs.

Corporations like us to innovate and they compliment us for producing good results. The participants ask to return to continue studying with us.

Companies reach out to us, we do not advertise or solicit corporations to gain employee training contracts. When approached, we write and provide the contract.

In this manner we try to integrate employeed training into the wider realm of adult education instead of replicating school house classes.

The only thing we don't eliminate in the process is the coercive element of job training. When an employer wants job-holders to learn a skill, they must do or die.

Before going on to the next section, it's important to note that Mariko and I advertise very successfully by placing only a small, hand-written note on a single bulletin board.

All that happens thereafter is word-of-mouth advertising, including the corporate courses.

Thus, when an electric company enquires about us, I first think it's calling because we've forgotten to pay our electric bill.

WORD SPREAD

"What we've got here is a failure to communicate."

The marginal product?

If adult education is considered important, as a means or as an end in itself, it includes the planning of effective marketing campaigns designed to attract the largest number of adult learners.

Even private companies with only marginal interest in adult education, mainly as a source of corporate profits, spare no expense to bring in the maximum number of adult learners as paying customers.

Prime examples of these companies in recent decades include the highly profitable L.B.E. (Language Business Establishments) with their extensive advertising campaigns.

In the past, one L.B.E. offered Céline Dion albums and other promotional gifts for adults who signed up to study.

Such gifts are well within L.B.E. advertising budgets, which are also business expense tax write-offs.

The L.B.E. collect fortunes from adult learners around the world. The L.B.E. have to hire more employees to keep up with the demand for expensive private and group sessions.

With this proven example of successful advertising, why do publicly run night schools for adult learners continue to lag so far behind and fail to attract enough learners to fill all classes available?

Night school could be helping to finance the day school.

Night school is organized and run by government-financed public schooling institutions with full access to day school's large physical infrastructure network.

In the context of advertising, the schooling infrastructure is an asset that can be exploited in an appropriate and positive way.

Unlike private companies, night school does not need to pay all the costs of starting from the ground up and building a whole new infrastructure before advertising.

If night school employed a core and administrative staff of adult educators, it would also have the adult course quality control capabilities that it needs.

The actual and potential night school advantages thus far exceed those of the private companies providing marginal adult education.

In serving the public interest rather than private financial profit, the goal of effective night school marketing should be to maximize learning opportunities for the largest number of adult learners, not to bring in the absolute minimum number of people necessary for "achievable goals" and to cover a basic budget.

Unfortunately, for generations, promoting adult education in the schooling system night school facilities is stymied by very feeble, minimal, and token advertising.

It's a far cry from all known highly successful product and services advertising campaigns.

They are designed by aggressive merchandisers who need to either sell or to face going out of business.

Night school advertising shows no such feeling of urgency, necessity, keenness, or zealous devotion toward selling adult education to a maximum number of actual and potential adult learners.

In the private sector, the lacklustre results of night school advertising would result in the termination of the administrative personnel responsible and the cancellation of contracts with advertising firms.

Night school somehow considers maximizing the number of people benefiting from lifelong learning an unprofitable venture and investment?

Maximizing access to continuing adult education is such a low priority for the schooling system that it isn't worth making the best efforts to actively and energetically promote it?

Advancing people and societies comes from encouraging lifelong adult learning.

People and societies which do not advance can only decline, fail, fall, and disappear.

Through lifelong adult learning, people gain better skills.

There is a more thoughtful and self-fulfilled adult population that can make better choices in all aspects of life, including basics such as nourishment.

Preordaining failure?

Since the closed schooling system is based on a captive audience of students, administrators from that system automatically behave as if night school course promotion isn't really that necessary.

Advertising can be extremely low-key, low budget, and passive.

News features about this year's night school classes can be arranged in exchange for paid advertising of classes in the same news media. That's not old school, it's ancient.

The closed system teacher and institution are ill-equipped for the hard work of offering appropriate adult courses and persuading people to sign up for them.

I get the impression from advertising and course offerings that, by and large:

1) Many instructors and administrators of adult night schools have no professional training, work experience, knowledge, or real interest in the field of adult education.

and

2) People having no knowledge of commercial advertising are responsible for arranging advertising campaigns for adult night schools.

The result is that many courses are doomed to failure at the pre-enrolment stage.

Regular customers may show up every year, out of seasonal habit, but most of the much larger pool of potential course participants isn't interested in a pre-ordained course lineup. Or they don't know it exists.

Advertising for the courses is, all too often, no more than two pages of plain, broadsheet newspaper, covered with mostly dull shades of ink with letters printed in small, unobtrusive, and bland fonts.

Little words are separated by tiny boxes with very neatly organized slightly larger, unexciting, unattractive, dull headings, such as "craft class".

This is not the work of professional news headline writers and editors.

Nor is it the product of advertising pros in firms responsible for highly successful mass media sales campaigns.

An interesting, perhaps alluring course heading and description may be buried somewhere in the columns and rows of tombstone head listings.

But who will bother trying to hunt for good courses in the inky sea of blandness? Life is too busy and short.

Although not without organization, the course listss appear to be randomly ordered in hodgepodge fashion, making finding a desired course even more difficult.

If the bland motif is writ-in-stone and not negotiable, because "We have always done it that way." why not simply put courses in alphabetical order by subject area?

Maybe that will cut costs by compressing the ad to a single page instead of two.

There will also be at least a few errors and typing mistakes in the ads, probably a result of boredom on the part of the people charged with preparing the dullness for publication.

Proof reading this type of advertising is tedious and hardly seems worth the effort because so few people are expected to read it?

For the publishers of this worst seller, the annual school board night school advertising is nonetheless a guaranteed revenue source coming from a government department.

What profit-seeking media would reject a guaranteed annual source of income?

Just submit it. The media will happily and uncritically take the money, no questions asked.

The apparent lack of interest and budget money for editing this form of advertising says that working very hard to encourage more people to participate in adult education is an unimportant and very low priority.

Nobody is willing to devote more than a token effort to attracting more adult learners and persuading them to take all sorts of courses?

The result is not a product of a long history of highly successful advertising experience and research, or of excellent advertising skills well applied.

It's very unlike typical commercial ad campaigns created by advertisers trying very hard to sell a product or service.

If the night school ads most commonly used during most of my lifetime to date were the product of a private corporation devoted to financial gain, that company might be under investigation for placing ads entirely for tax write-off purposes or as part of a scheme to launder money by moving funds through mass media channels.

All of the wasted money, cyberspace, ink, energy, and paper go under a lifeless, unintriguing, unattractive, non-attracting, smaller-than-life banner headline reading:

"Such-and-such School Board Winter Evening Classes" or "Night School".

They can well be called offerings, in the funerary sense.

Why not just staple a sheet of white typed paper on an electric pole? It would probably attract more attention.

Angry complaints from the power company would get more free publicity for night school too.

In a world filled with action, danger, and intrigue; exciting and amazing attractions, inventions, entertainment, and stunning events; it's a wonder that anyone would ever look at night school advertising.

Night school ads in newspapers with a declining readership will soon be in the recycle bin, used for drying soaked shoes, or folded to line the bottoms of bird cages.

Drab night school ads delivered to "in-boxes" will soon be deleted, declared junk mail and spam, or destined for "unsubscribe" and "block sender" clicks.

Why not try an advanced, present day approach to advertising instead of plodding along as if printing and typing were new inventions and nobody yet knew much about how to use advertising to its maximum effectiveness?

Why do schooling institutions continue to use a form of newspaper advertising that's the only option during the earliest years of the printing press but not today?

It's amazing that anyone with any sense of cost-effectiveness today is willing to pay a newspaper to print extremely outmoded throwaway ads for adult night school classes.
Schooling institutions may try to explain away the waste by saying they have very restricted budgets for night school advertising, so they can't afford to pay for better ads.

With that severe restriction, why advertise at all? Save money by closing night schools altogether.

Isn't the budget excuse a confession that an organization is knowingly squandering the very little money it has by throwing it away on advertising that it knows is a waste of money?

If it doesn't know that, it's even worse off.

This foolish waste doesn't excuse newspapers, printing shops, website designers, or others for accepting almost useless ads.

I get the impression they show no apparent bad conscience for taking taxpayer's money for ads that won't produce substantial results.

Newspapers, printers, and others know the educational institution ads are outmoded and ineffective compared with the great variety of proven effective advertising formats and styles now available.

Media know the difference because while they're accepting poor night school ads for many years, they're also publishing great advertising that works every day.

So it's appalling that, year after year, decade after decade, so many newspaper advertising departments, printers, etc. continue to accept the same old night school ads.

In exchange for public monies, the papers, printers, website designers, etc. are publishing adult course advertising that is inappropriate and ineffective in attracting most potential adult learners for most courses offered.

The papers, printers, website designers, etc. should be paying back the public, including their customers, by helping public educational institutions to improve their ads.

To be perfectly honest, the papers, printers, etc. could at least tell the night school administrators that they're wasting their money.

Smart newspaper advertising departments, printers, etc. could go much further. They could suggest advertising alternatives that would work.

They could offer to help the public schooling institutions to improve the ads for a nominal fee.

It would be good publicity for the newspapers, printers, etc., showing that they're contributing to helping publicly-funded education.

In future years, the newspapers, printers, etc. could charge more for ads because the adult course providers would be attracting more learners.

Night school would gain more revenue and so increase the amount of money available for advertising.

A clever newspaper, printer, etc. could do much more, in the mutual interest of both adult education and the media itself.

The paper, printer, etc. could offer to improve publicly-funded night school advertising as a public service, free of charge, one time only.

In exchange, the schooling institutions could agree to let the media advertise their generosity.

Institutions could publicly thank the media for their assistance by including their names and logos on adult course ads, posters, plaques, etc. displayed inside and outside of institutional buildings.

Governments could recognize and reward the advertising media's benevolence, free service, and voluntary contribution to adult education, by granting the media a special tax write-off for the costs of improving adult course advertising.

Unfortunately, to date, the newspaper advertising departments, printers, etc. don't seem to give any thought to helping to improve adult course advertising.

Newspapers, printers, etc. seem much more interested in making the maximum profit from the schooling institutions' ignorance.

The newspapers and printers are behaving like any other business that's only trying to gain the most money for the least effort.

They don't seem to understand that it's far more profitable to invest in making societies better, by actively supporting and promoting adult education.

Better societies can provide businesses with a larger number of more affluent customers.

So long as schooling systems, newspapers, printers, etc. continue to publish mediocre advertising for night school, adult education will continue to languish far behind other priorities and activities in the daily lives of most people.

Bland, unappealing night school advertising can never compete with the professional, riveting, flashy advertising typical of today's communications media.

Seasonal adult education advertising will continue to be so drab, low key, unimaginative, and lacking in innovation that night school will remain in its present dark state indefinitely.

Plodding through night school ads will continue to be an act of desperation, a last resort, or an idle afterthought for many people.

They put the adult course ads aside for reading some time later, if no one throws them in the garbage or they don't get deleted from the in-box by mistake.

Widespread attention span deficiency kicks in.

If reading the adult course ads does happen at all, it may be long after the news, sports, weather, feature stories, and glossy advertising flyers are on the way to the recycling box.

The course may be cancelled or finished by the time many potential learners get around to reading the ads.

Thus most people probably find out about courses by mere chance, not thanks to an effective course advertising campaign.

For many people, reading the night school ad is not something to do with enthusiasm.

It's not a pleasure, an adventure, or a treasure hunt. It's a routine act to struggle through once or twice a year, if ever.

At the same time, the poor calibre of advertising and promotion is likely to obscure and conceal the larger choice of courses, including ones not offered to adults when they were pupils and students.

Advertising campaigns created to put a box of low nutrition, high sugar content, highly processed breakfast cereal on every kitchen table are far superior to night school advertising campaigns. Likewise caffeine ads.

When hundreds of millions of adults wake up every morning they are bombarded with cereal and coffee commercials, not adult education commercials.

Here are some suggestions for mind-nourishing alternatives to the daily bombardment.

Good advertising can make adult education the healthy addiction, unlike sugar and caffeine.

"Good morning everybody! It's time to make your life better with adult education! Call this number now! Start improving your life right away! ..."

"It's almost time for the news headlines. It's always time for adult education. Start now! Call this number... Get more ADED!... And bring a friend."

Commuters in transit could be seeing ads like these:

"Another day, another dollar? Get more ADED! aded.org"

"Get away to it all? Get more ADED! aded.org"

"Feeling down & out? Need something ADED! aded.org"

<u>BUT!</u>

No matter how good or lacklustre the advertising, adult education depends on the commitment of the society, the adult learners, and the adult educators.

Both the general public and the elite need to be prepared to embrace and support adult education as an essential public service deserving massive public and private investment.

The investment will be in furthering and maintaining the coming of a truly democratic system and society.

Adult learners' experiences in adult education will result in an increasing demand for the achievement of that goal.

Adult learners must be heard at all times, from the earliest moments of programme planning to the final session of each programme.

Adult learners are the chief executive officers of adult education.

Adult learners have to be the leaders who adult educators are constantly asking what, when, where, and why they want to learn.

Legions of adult educators, veterans and newcomers to the field, need to be professionally trained, supported, and recruited and supported through public and private funding.

Adult educators will include every person facilitating adult learners in their efforts to pursue the interests they express through constant consultation with adult educators.

The desired outcome and achievement is a society in which everyone has the opportunity to learn whatever s/he wishes to learn for whatever purposes s/he determines.

This covers every type of adult learning activity both inside and outside of formal institutional settings, institutions, and infrastructure.

Adult education is a massive undertaking which must not exclude any adult anywhere and must include every adult everywhere.

These efforts to improve and further adult education will require an enormous amount of dedication and effort to bring about one of the most significant achievements in human history - a population having positive and widely beneficial goals and a population with the ability and means to achieve them.

ILL-PREPARED HOSTS AT THE MARGINS

Many types of organizations offer adult education, for both public profit and private profit. Some organizations are more disadvantaged than others in this work.

Perhaps the worst off is the municipal school system which devotes most of its resources to its sole area of expertise, child and adolescent formal schooling.

Thus the school system is essentially a top-down dictatorial organization in which the pupils and students are simply pawns to be moved around by the ruling administrators and teachers.

This is an entirely inappropriate background and preparation for adult education, which is essentially and by necessity democratic.

Adult learners are not compelled by law to attend schools and to obey those ruling the school system.

If adult learners are confronted with the dictatorial school system of their pre-adult lives they are less likely to learn and more likely to leave.

While living in St. John's, Newfoundland and Labrador my partner Mariko and I are encountering people who have difficulty teaching adults because they have training and experience in school teaching alone.

Aside from the clear differences between teaching school children and helping employed adults to learn, there are problems in the school system itself which hinder and impede school teachers' attempts to try to teach adults.

In these attempts, school teachers I observe seem lost without the systems' off-the-shelf, fixed package "teaching materials" and institutionalized pupil-student audience.

In the system gives the impression that the materials are doing the teaching instead of teaching being a product of the teachers' observations and intelligent minds.

The school teachers we observe struggling with adult education seem challenged because there's no fixed, set, legislated curriculum package, teachers' guide, text book, school structure, and routine to fall back on.

More troubling for the school teachers is that every adult learner has a great variety of different life experiences going far beyond those of children and adolescents.

In many cases, if not all, the adult learners' experiences also exceed those of the "teacher", i.e. the person officially responsible for and getting paid to run a course for adults.

The school teacher is at most an equal with the learners for the first time. S/he must recognize this apparent fact and treat learners as his/her equals for the first time.

This can be humbling and difficult to except because it completely contradicts all of the school teacher's prior training and experience.

For the first time in her/his life, a school teacher has to cope with the fact that learners have much to teach the "teacher".

They can't be put in an inferior position or brow-beaten. They can't be forced to accept only the perspectives and interpretations of a teacher, a text, and the system.

The school teacher has no built-in age advantage, statutory authority, or veteran worker seniority power to support or justify ruling over adult learners.

They are likely to know at least as much and sometimes more than s/he does.

Both public profit and private profit organizations involved in adult education can be similarly ill-prepared and have great difficulty in their efforts, if any, to adapt to adult learners.

In effect, the basic facts of adult education mean that school teachers in night school are rendered as poorly prepared and ineffective as L.B.E. (Language Business

Establishment) unprofessional staff hired with the expectation that being "native speakers" of a language will somehow make them instant language teachers.

A certificate in elementary or secondary school teaching doesn't prepare a school teacher to facilitate adult learning.

As a Montréal adult educator points out to a group of visiting adult education students that I'm a part of, we are "androgogues" not "pedagogues".

We don't have a set curriculum. We have flexible, alterable, and adaptable programmes and courses for adult learners.

Instead of requiring teaching certificates that don't prepare staff to teach adult language learners, L.B.E. base their staff hiring practices on the job applicant's first language.

"Native speakers" get first and usually only preference in hiring. The "native" origins of the applicant can also be a factor.

An apologetic personnel manager in Sapporo politely tells me that he can only hire people with U.K. accents. At least he's honest.

I don't find this bias in a U.S.-based L.B.E. I know. Some staff there have U.K. and Australian accents.

Regardless of the accepted accent at L.B.E., being born a "native speaker" of a language doesn't prepare anyone to facilitate adult language learners.

One of the L.B.E. where I work in years past admits this fact, perhaps inadvertently, by training "native speaker" staff not to make common "native speaker" grammatical mistakes while attempting to teach their first language.

"Native speaker equivalent" staff are also hired, which often means people who can teach a language better because they don't make the common "native speaker" mistakes. They can probably spell better too.

It's a shame that neither L.B.E. nor night schools train their staff and teachers how to facilitate adult learning.

But unlike public schooling's ill-prepared forays into night school, the L.B.E. and publishers associated with them make their fortunes by blurring the differences between the prepared and the unprepared for teaching adults.

Copying the schooling system, the L.B.E. use "text books", but more expensive ones with lots of colour, flashy covers, and illustrations.

These L.B.E. and publisher invented materials can be the authentic products of actual linguistics or language teachers who are commissioned and well-paid.

Materials come with promises to enhance learning through printed, recorded, and electronic means.

For many years, Oxford University Press publishes books used by L.B.E. staff and sold to L.B.E. customers.

Equally true, at one point, one of the famous U.S.-based L.B.E. belongs to a non-university-based publishing house. Another L.B.E. uses the name of a famous encyclopedia.

Since a publisher's prime goal is to sell its publications, L.B.E. can be useful. L.B.E. are an additional advertising channel to market publications.

Products from various publishers may also come with good teacher's guides and a complete curriculum plan too.

But for the L.B.E., the materials are like the "native speaker" staff. They are mainly used as props to attract paying customers.

Materials can sell like magic potions guaranteed to result in instant language learning.

But the L.B.E. remain devoted to their own private financial profit, not to providing adult education. It's just a sideline, much like night school for the schooling system.

But appearances remain important to the L.B.E.

One of the L.B.E. boasts to potential customers that the head "teacher" is listening to every "lesson" using a microphone in the ceiling of every "class" room.

A few blocks away, another L.B.E. has video screen monitors in its customer lobby area displaying that there is a camera in every "class" room, implying quality control.

This L.B.E. surveillance is in place long before "security" placed cameras and microphones everywhere to monitor everyone.

However, like the "security" of more recent history, what's the point if the people listening and watching have no idea what's really going on in front of the cameras and microphones?

Without the appropriate professional training, how can the observers be any more than eavesdroppers who can't tell the difference between education and entertainment and who misinterpret what they hear or see as "suspicious behaviour"?

On a far less technological level, when I ask for a piece of chalk to help me teach, the "head teacher" at one L.B.E. tells me not to use the small chalk boards located in every "class" room.

He says, "The chalk boards are only there to make it look like a real school."

Besides, what good are the props when the L.B.E. "native speaker" staff by and large lack the professional teacher training of any kind that's required to make use any of the props to effectively facilitate adult learning?

Fortunately for the staff, the L.B.E. only needs staff to appear to follow a book and to try to appear to be professional teachers without actually being so.

If customers lose interest and doze off, staff can get friendly and start playing "hangman" or other games for a break, and to keep things lively.

Or staff can talk away the time and ask customers to answer questions about the customers' first language. At least the staff might learn a language this way.

Unlike L.B.E. staff, professional school teachers must actually follow a book or other teaching aid approved by a school board or other bureaucracy.

But the teaching aid is the central feature in both regular schooling and L.B.E. customer paid encounters with native speakers.

Professional school teachers are trained and programmed into complete dependence on bureaucratic rule and submission to publishing committee decisions on texts in whatever form they are published, books or not.

The published material is not the only feature that professional school teachers and L.B.E. staff involved in adult night school have in common.

L.B.E. staff, like professional school teachers are not appropriately trained to provide adult education.

School teachers involved in adult night school are no better prepared to manage adult education than L.B.E. staff are to teach adults or anyone else a language.

L.B.E. staff and professional school teachers have nothing to fall back on when they encounter adult learners.

Essentially, they are in the same predicament, even though L.B.E. staff are most obviously starting from zero.

When a professional school teacher encounters adult learners, school teacher training and experience are almost all for nought.

School teachers are stripped of all their familiar and comfortable school teaching supports.

Contrary to all their previous teaching work, they suddenly have nothing and no one to fall back on, including themselves.

They lose all the predetermined/prearranged hierarchical choices that they have had to abide by in the past. They have no practical adult education experience to draw upon.

They truly don't know what to do. They don't know how to plan and provide an education programme that is appropriate for adult learners.

Perhaps recognizing their professional deficiencies, at least some child and adolescent teachers take an adult education graduate course with me at university.

Without at least that training, the result is... nothing.

When school teachers struggle and flounder, adult learners in night schools will find themselves left to fend for themselves, using their own resources just as they do to cope with most events in their lives.

If they learn anything in night school, it's almost entirely due to their own patience, persistence, and efforts to overcome the handicaps imposed by the schooling system.

Adult learning thus becomes essentially an exercise in self-education.

The same applies to L.B.E. customers.

At night school, the school teacher in the room may be little more than window dressing and/or a make work project for school teachers or others seeking supplementary income.

Expert teachers in specific areas of study are another matter. They may fall under the expression, "Those who can do. Those who can't teach."

But they are probably better described as people who can do something well but who don't always know how to teach adults.

Like "native speaker" status, expertise in any field, including school teaching, does not make a person a competent or appropriate teacher in adult education.

S/he may be very eloquent and/or superb in his/her field of expertise, but entirely incompetent in training adult learners.

I see this problem in at least one university classroom in a regular course for students in an undergraduate degree programme.

One of my older professors quietly and confidently presents himself as an intellectual, an established expert, and at times a friendly person.

However, much like two of my secondary school science teachers, he seems to believe that he can successfully convey and impart learning mainly by assigning students to read passages from a single required reading book.

Although it is very unlikely that he actually believes this to be true, his approach to attempting to teach the subject matter reveals only that he lacks effective teaching skills.

Perhaps he lacks the people skills to attempt to truly help students or he is too proud to critically evaluate his approach to teaching.

To make matters worse, he probably has the lifelong employment guarantee called tenure, given his age and position title.

Only students in his course will suffer the consequences of his minimal teaching strategy, not him. He can repeat the same mistakes for the rest of his tenure, unimpeded.

A course in how to teach young adult learners would help him, but none is available to him unless he enrols in the adult education department.

He probably won't do so, perhaps out of pride or his unperceived ignorance of his own shortcomings.

In the realm of adult education for adult learners who are not in an academic or degree programme and who are attending night classes, the variety of expertise among people working as teachers is quite divergent.

Yet there is no apparent permanent and ongoing training programme arranged especially for any of them to help them acquire any of the skills required to teach adult learners.

These experts walk into classroom settings knowing only their fields of expertise. They know nothing about adult education.

They may work for many years offering their night school classes because many people like the subject matter, regardless of who is responsible for teaching it.

Some people might be signing up for the course simply because they admire an expert or like her/him personally.

Or the person taking the course likes one of the other students.

The experts can thus end up repeating the same teaching errors until they become calcified.

Whether or not few or any people learn anything by registering in the class seems to be unimportant.

So long as people keep signing up for the course and paying the school board fees, the expert will continue to have a job. The bureaucracy won't cancel the course.

It's the same model of "success" and criterion for continuity used by the L.B.E. to justify offering the same staff for the same "courses" for adults who want to learn languages.

Never mind the fact that they return year after year and don't improve their language schools. That's "their fault", not the L.B.E.'s.

Although a night school course too is theoretically supposed to help adult learners, it can end up being no more effective than exposing potential language learners to non-professional and inept "native speaker" staff at L.B.E.

L.B.E. staff need training that their employer has little or no interest or competence in providing. It's apparently also an added and unwanted business expense and tax write-off.

At most, newly hired staff will be trained in "applying the method", not in teaching adult learners. "The method is for all ages."

The same staff use the same books for children, adolescent, and adult customers.

At the L.B.E., making a fast fortune takes precedence over providing actual language education. L.B.E. profits increase, until someone says "The Emperor has no clothes."

I only see that happen once to date, when one of the biggest L.B.E. in Nippon has to close down and go out of business after customers complain to the national government.

Another simply changes its name before the government gets involved. It survives through the rebranding.

School teachers and experts offering courses for adult learners in night school lack the L.B.E. private profit motive, but they need teacher training in adult education just as badly as L.B.E. staff need to learn how to teach languages.

Otherwise, adult night school becomes largely a supplementary fund-raising project for the school boards, not a means of offering the best possible learning opportunities for adults.

Why not invest in adult education and make some effort to improve night school for all adult learners?

Since night school lacks the amoral profit-maximizing motive of the L.B.E., night school should invest in and use only administrators, instructors, planners, and programmes rooted in adult education, not childhood-adolescent schooling.

ORIGINS OF THE PROBLEM

All of the parties involved in offering the adult courses described in the forgoing writing are at fault, including me.

Mariko and I simply try to fit into a system which is inherently likely to fail for most people offering most non-academic programme, non-compulsory, and non-credit courses.

But the institutional approach is the greatest contributor to the problem.

It's largely top down. It implies that adult education is neither devoted to improving people's lives nor a part of a democratic system.

Institutions and potential night school teachers dictate what courses will be offered, by whom, when, and where. There is no public participation in any of this planning.

This non-participation is rooted in the larger realm of school boards and other educational institutions.

They have traditionally restricted public contact and participation in schooling to PTA meetings, buying tickets for school shows, and putting out money during fundraising drives.

The school system shows little or no interest in finding out about and learning from the schooling experiences of parents who now find their children subjected to virtually the same top-down system.

Ironically, the adult parents now discover they are almost as helpless as their children. Parents are outsiders who are powerless to take effective action to improve schooling.

In some cases, this is because the parents almost humbly defer to the schools rulers' "professional" superiority. What do I know? I'm not a teacher.

In other cases, frustrated parents only offer angry complaints instead of presenting well-researched proposals or organizing a strong parents' lobby outside the PTA structure, to push for improving the school system.

Emotional outbursts about the way their children are treated can be dismissed as annoying parental prejudices. How can you treat _my_ child that way?

Docile parents can be completely ignored. Complaining parents can be grudgingly tolerated.

But the parents' own personal schooling experiences, and their insider views on it, are of no concern or importance to the supreme rulers of the school system.

The school system treats adult learners as extensions of this tradition of institution-centred schooling.

From this narrow perspective of adult education, night school students are no more than grownup children who are former elementary school pupils and secondary school students.

They have a history of being controlled in schooling and they can be reminded of that history through night school planning that excludes them.

Is it any wonder that night classes are held in the same dreary, sterile buildings and small desks that adults used when they were children and adolescents?

Night school must be schooling again. It must always fit in and show its conformity with, obedience to, and respect for the dictates of the schooling system.

Adult learners must respond again to exactly the same bells, buzzers, whistles, and/or musical notes that ran their younger institutionalized lives.

Adult learners are thus required to behave much like salivating Pavlovian dogs, but with no guarantee of getting their minds nourished in night school.

Not too long ago, one provincial cabinet minister expressed this approach to adult learners in an even more disparaging manner.

He said, without fear of losing any votes, that adults returning to school are merely going for "a second kick at the can" to make up for past academic failures or lackings.

He was trying to justify budget cuts to continuing education programmes.

Perhaps unaware of or indifferent to the world-changing potential, depth, and diversity of adult education, and its incalculable value to societies, he was saying -

Why fund the people who didn't finish or get enough out of school the first time? Why throw good money after bad?

He didn't want to encourage people like my dad and part-time university students to seek learning opportunities?

Perhaps he wanted to re-entrench his rule over the "ignorant masses" by protecting his elite status as someone with more advanced formal education.

Maybe he was simply power hungry.

This type of politics does nothing to improve the state of adult learners and the quality of adult education in night school.

The closest that adult learners get to participating in night school planning is if and when they vote in municipal elections for school board candidates.

This participation is short-lived and the influence of voters on night school is tenuous at best.

The candidate choices are often no more than former or current school board employees, including teachers. They promise to increase or cut the budget for schools.

Electoral campaigns that mention night school classes probably never happen.

Since municipal voter turnout is very low and the night school budgeting process is far removed from direct public scrutiny, most people are completely excluded from planning all aspects of night school adult education.

Potential night school participants have only two ways of exercising their very restricted impact on night schools.

They can either not sign up for the courses offered to them or they can drop out and forfeit the money they pay in advance for courses.

The results could be more than cancelled courses.

An institution may decide to reduce choices further and to offer only academic credit courses subsidized by the school board.

The role of night school students is given low institutional priority and short shift, except as a source of extra funding for the school board's actual priorities.

Popular courses are merely good sources of revenue. If a course is popular, milk it for all it's worth.

The subject could be a fad of the moment, but it could continue for several years.

Night school course planners, including me in Canadian towns, treat potential and actual students as if they were merely present to learn what they are told to learn in classes that they have no part in planning.

Worse, night students are treated as if they were present to provide jobs for school teachers without full-time employment who are only adding to their résumés for school board positions.

I have never studied for or wanted one of those positions and, despite my attempted complicity in the top-down system, the school bureaucracy far exceeds me in arrogance.

Schools are rooted and founded in a concept of dictatorial institutions.

Pupils and students are present to obediently learn or to disobediently ignore and drop out of what the school board and provincial government tell them to learn. Why should adult learners expect better treatment?

So why should adult learners expect or receive a democratic say in what they want to learn?

The school system decides everything, publishes a list of the courses that teachers want to offer and that only the school bureaucracy can approve.

The school system tells potential night students to sign up and pay for anything on the predetermined and preordained list. Take it or leave it.

NOT HAVING A CHOICE

Schooling institutions seem to have little or no interest in asking any potential learners what they want to learn, when they want to learn it, and where they want to learn it.

But sometimes, after the institutional priorities of building, room, and maintenance are settled, and the almost random selection of courses and instructors is complete, and just before the advertising is finalized and the deadline for submitting ads passes, some institutions might do one other thing.

Institutions might ask someone to make up a questionnaire asking people what kind of adult courses they might want to take.

The emphasis in the question and the answer is on the word "might".

Neither the institution nor the potential participant needs to make any commitment whatsoever. The institution might offer a course and some people might take it.

Unfortunately, the questionnaire is thus much like the advertising, i.e. neither well-designed nor effective, and probably an almost entirely useless formality of going through the motions of appearing interested or responsible.

The questionnaire may be no more than an attempt at very low key, almost invisible supplementary advertising. It's all about "going through the motions".

Or it may be a mere political strategy to justify and support the institution's budget and already planned courses. "Fund us. We care. We're performing a public service."

It's can be no more than an exercise in giving others the impression that the night school is actively seeking public input and participation to improve things.

To ease "analysis" of the results, questions are closed, asking people to choose only from a list of courses already provided by the institution.

It's the old "multiple choice" exam in which you have a 25% change of getting "the right answer" of "the best answer".

Mariko and I are familiar with this type of "participation" in planning. In the U.K. we take part in a day-long planning session for a municipal library in one town.

Whenever a member of the public comes up with an interesting suggestion to improve the library, it is ignored.

The people running the session respond by emphasizing that participants must limit themselves to the topics listed by the session organizers. "We" know what's best!

At least a night school questionnaire might provide a small blank space on the last page of the questionnaire (to save paper or kilobytes), titled "Other comments."

If it's an on-line questionnaire, you must strictly observe the "character" limit determined unilaterally by the web master planners.

The questionnaire won't have completely open-ended questions, such as "What courses do you suggest?" or "Do you have any suggestions about where and when courses should be held?"

Whatever is written in the blank space of the questionnaire will get far less attention than the closed questions that are unilaterally worded by the questionnaire makers.

The institution clerk burdened with actually looking at and reporting the official results of the questionnaire, will probably skim over the blank space.

S/he is only looking for key words supporting decisions and choices already made by the institution for the people signing up for courses.

Why not have a key to cover the closed question answers too, like the ones used for schooling "multiple choice tests".

In test-marking, a key saves school teachers' time and money, as well as pre-empting clear and comprehensive evaluation thinking, such as -

In the real world there is no one "best" answer to any question. Why deliberately try to persuade people to believe that there really is a "right" answer to every question?

In questionnaires, a "multiple choice" key could help institutions to quickly find only the closed question responses which agree with the choices the institution prefers, i.e. the "best" ones.

Asking questions is not the same as listening to answers and acting upon them.

Abstract intent to use the word participate is also not the same as participation.

In Rio de Janeiro, some people say that they would like to be adventurers like me, but…

In Miyazaki, various people tell Mariko and me that they would like to learn a language, but…

"But" is a great excuse for total inaction in life.

An authentic open-ended survey is a lot more work but it can produce far better results for participants in life than a questionnaire based on ignoring suggestions and pushing through a premeditated agenda to rule the world.

SURVEYING THE SITUATION

Even after nothing works in Dyingtown, I get a unique opportunity to try to improve the night school system.

By chance, someone I know at the First Nations Friendship Centre invites me to fill out a survey form on night schooling at the local community college.

A regular daytime college student group develops a questionnaire to ask potential adult students about the college night school course offerings.

I write some thoughtful phrases to try to influence the community college toward democratizing its system of planning and offering courses for adult learners.

I'm very keen on making a contribution toward helping night school improve.

I use the questionnaire to write as much as I can in the blank spaces and backs of each sheet of paper.

I explain in detail how an organization offering adult continuing education classes could make an effort to encourage public participation in creating a list of what courses should be offered along with the when, where, etc.

Questionnaires to potential adult learners would have to be completely open-ended, with no preconceived notions of what people want to learn, where they can learn, and when they can learn.

First ask people responding to the survey to make a list of things they'd like to learn about.

Ask people to state their preferences, first, second, & third choices for time of year, days, and times for taking adult courses.

Then start developing preliminary course plans, schedules, and advertising content that fit what and when local people actually want to learn.

The resulting course list and schedule would be a direct reflection of the potential participants and say exactly what they want instead of merely mirroring the dictates of institutions and instructors.

If this isn't a goal of adult education, what is?

I follow-up by writing to the college president suggesting an open-ended questionnaire, including an area where potential learners can include a wish list of courses they would like to take.

I emphasize my ideas and how they could be implemented to improve the adult night school by encouraging more public participation.

I offer to provide more help to improve local adult education as a professional consultant, for a fee.

The only reaction is immediate, terse, and negative. The college administrator in Dyingtown is offended by my suggestions and offer to help.

He seems to take my comments on the problems of all night courses that I'm aware of, in many different places, as a personal attack on him.

Instead of thanking me for taking the time to do much more than check off answers in the questionnaire, he chastises me for sharing my ideas with someone out of town.

He disowns the questionnaire that I fill out, saying that it's only a student project and he is "very disturb" (sic) that I write about it to his boss.

We hear no more from him, his boss, or his employer.

My questionnaire writing says nothing about him or his position. Nor do I single out the community college itself as a unique and bad example of night school planning.

Unfortunately, it's all too typical.

Why not show up the others by doing something much better than them?

Unfortunately, input to improve things is not wanted, not welcome, and not acted upon.

There is no change whatsoever in the approach of night school institutions to planning their courses in Dyingtown.

I apologize to the administrator for my heinous "crime". But that's the last I hear from the Dyingtown adult night school people.

Is my recommendation for a democratic approach to planning adult education programmes so outlandish and absolutely impossible to try?

Or is this just a wider illustration of the fact that Dyingtown is not just one place or location - It is a state of mind?

In subsequent years, everywhere that I look beyond that town there is still a list of courses dictated and published in the same way and form, even on the Internet.

Ads I see look as if web site designers are told to do the equivalent of scanning the old newspaper ad format flyers and reproducing them as web page clones.

The only additions may be animation and links. The top-down approach and substance are the same as ever.

Public participation continues to be nil.

The participation of potential students is still limited to not signing up for the courses advertised; or, to dropping out and losing all their money by not getting a full refund when the courses fail to satisfy them.

Somehow the institutional and school boards continue to blindly fund this undemocratic approach to adult night school offerings.

The assumption may be that this form of top-down planning requires minimum effort and is cheaper than a democratic approach.

The larger assumption is that most people will not take part in adult night school classes except for the high school dropouts, the employeed sent by employers, and the lonely people desperate for social interaction.

So there is no need to improve or democratize anything.

Or, as the townsfolk say to Dr. Verner long ago, "We don't want to change."

Classes can simply be cancelled if not enough people want to enrol and pay fees. It's all about and only about numbers, largely monetary ones, not adult education.

Some courses do survive. But all too often these are the adult classes that night school administrators simply describe as "what's always/usually popular".

By coincidence, it's always/usually what night school prefers to offer too? After all, it is night "school", with the emphasis on school schooling.

But isn't public education in the public schooling system non-profit in the financial sense?

So why merely live off the minimum income from the easiest classes to fill?

Why not make a good effort to fill all the other types of classes that can bring in more money to cover their costs too and in so doing enable night school to expand?

Education ministries, school boards, and schools are not created to make money. They are funded by taxpayers' money to further education.

Taxpayers include night school students who want to further their education.

The people responsible for education don't want to risk learning?

They don't want to risk learning how to do things better and more effectively to help a larger percentage of the population to learn?

With such a minimal approach to education in mind, I'm now adding something to my Dyingtown questionnaire answers.

Most if not all night school classes should be subsidized like the rest of the school system and offered free of charge.

The only condition attached to this public funding project is that the potential and actual night school adult learners will lead the course planning process.

School board representatives and bureaucrats will help adult learners in this process, not manipulate, limit, or control them.

The learners will also have an equal role in screening and selecting the instructors.

Learner participation will help to determine whether or not instructors have the prerequisite skills and qualifications for working as adult educators.

How open is the applicant to ongoing democratic adult programme planning and replanning to adapt courses to the learners and their learning strategies?

Again, at present, night school learners can only influence the choice of teachers by not enrolling and by dropping out with or without complaints.

IN THE DEEP OF THE NIGHT SCHOOL

Marvin is one of my former fellow students in adult education. He becomes a dean at Vancouver Vocational Institute (VVI).

I think he's working there while studying with me. Maybe he's a dean then too.

We meet a few years later and have a very long conversation in his office.

Now he tells me how much older he is than I am. He takes on the look of a wise elder, saying he's 60. Suddenly I notice his wrinkles and the dark spots on his saggy arms.

Just as suddenly, his age disappears and his face brightens as he tells me that VVI came up with a night school plan that "made the place rock".

He says VVI decided to offer night school classes all night long. As a result, VVI was full of adult learners at all hour of the night. As Marvin explains it:

Some people just learn better at night. That's their peak time.

They come in with an energy that goes beyond all the expectations of the VVI decision-makers who throw upon the doors to adult learners of all hours and shifts.

It's an amazing story coming out of an ostensibly staid and conventional job-training public education institution that normally operates like regular schooling with regular hours.

I don t know how long this success story in risk-taking carries on.

But I do know what happens to Marvin.

Before we part, he asks me, with a very serious face and in a very grave tone, if I have thought about "the" future.

People who don't know me very well have some fantastic notions about my very fulfilling life, the wonders I experience, and the stimulating challenges I face "outside the main stream".

People who thus misread and misinterpret others have a great need for adult education, at least in my regard.

Martin is apparently giving me a stern, well-intentioned, and concerned warning about my "precarious" worldwide adventures.

I politely don't laugh in his face. He needs to do a lot of research instead of blindly jumping to easily disproven conclusions.

Nevertheless, not long after our long conversation, Marvin amazes and pleases me. He quits his guaranteed lifelong employment.

He leaves the very respectable and secure career position that's taking him to "the" future, and quickly becomes a very successful international adult education private contractor.

The last I hear from him, Marvin says he's enjoying his life more than ever before and making lots of money. He concludes by saying "I should have left VVI years ago."

DISCONTINUING EDUCATION

Wondering for a long time and finally getting around to look, Mariko and I enter a very small building across the street from the Memorial University main campus.

A sign outside says "Continuing Education".

Inside, on one of the four storeys labelled "Continuing Education" on the lobby floor directory, I ask someone in an office about programmes.

Mariko and I are doing some "professional" research, finding out if this department has any language courses either requiring or competing with us.

The person in the office tells me the department no longer exists.

She explains that the university decides it's not needed and its courses could be offered by the "private sector".

That's us.

She also says the small college down the road picks up some of the work.

At this point I make my little speech about lifelong learning and how important it is.

I say it's especially important now, with so many of the employed looking for work and with the huge numbers of people from the big "baby boom" generation either retiring or about to do so.

They want to do something productive and interesting with their remaining time.

Of course she agrees, but that does nothing about the weird decision by MUN's bosses.

The private sector and places down the road have always been involved in continuing education of one sort, and quality, or another.

It takes me back to Dyingtown and my critique of the way continuing education courses are selected, planned, offered, and advertised.

It's planned obsolescence instead of aggressively planning the expansion and proliferation of adult learning.

L.E.T.S.

After years of disappointing encounters with L.B.E., my partner Mariko and I break out on our own. We create L.E.T.S. (Language & Educational Training Services).

L.E.T.S. becomes our sole "employer". It belongs entirely to us alone.

I invent the name L.E.T.S. It's a much better alternative for Mariko, me, and our students. We all gain by eliminating the L.B.E. intermediary parasite.

Tuition and our income are based entirely on how much the L.B.E. pay us in the past out of the much larger sums collected from their customers.

One of the L.B.E. I work for claims it's the best in terms of employee salaries, paying one-third of the money it collects from customers.

So we save our students 66.6% of what they would pay "the best" paying L.B.E. arrangement and we get the same income.

What's far more important is that we are much better prepared than the average L.B.E. "teaching" staff.

We are an experienced and well-trained adult educator and an experienced and well-trained modern languages instructor.

We are very competent practitioners in language skill acquisition training.

Such people are very rare, if they exit at all, in the ranks of L.B.E. staff. I'm not aware of having ever met such a person at any of the L.B.E. where I work.

So our offering and tuition for students is an excellent value and bargain.

Beyond these very minimal and basic advantages of studying with Mariko and me, we offer language courses based on our students themselves, not based on what companies are trying to sell as "text books" and recordings.

We study our students before they study with us and while they are studying with us.

This begins in Miyazaki when Mariko interviews each potential student in his/her first language.

Aside from questions s/he may ask before starting a course with us, this is his/her final opportunity to speak her/his first language in our presence.

During Mariko's preliminary interview, she will determine the potential student's motivation and attitude toward language study, as well as his/her activities and interests in life.

If Mariko is satisfied with the student, we teach her/him. If not, we don't.

If the student fails to show the same motivation and attitude throughout his/her course, we asked her/him to leave. Course over.

If a student decides to leave, s/he can do so without hesitation.

S/he pays no admission fee, unlike the L.B.E., and s/he has no contract for a certain number of classes, months, or years, unlike the L.B.E. S/he loses no money for leaving.

Our only rule, from experience, is that a student has a unique month of studies, starting the date of her/his first class and ending on the fourth class. The calendar month is irrelevant. Four classes have to end within four weeks.

Most students remain with us for years and never quit. Very few leave and two give a month's notice.

Only one leaves suddenly, without warning, after years of studying with us. We don't know why. He continues to praise and recommend us to others.

We are unique in another way too. We are not pushing nation-state or linguistic stereotypes, absolutes, and myths. We do not support nationalism.

Our setting and courses use only examples we know from our Canadian experience.

I always say to Mariko that there are enough people out there pushing only the U.S. and U.K. We stick to what we know much more about, Canada.

Since anglophones and dictionaries in Canada use both U.S. and U.K. forms of English, our students have an additional advantage over their counterparts learning exclusively one or the other.

We also teach both of Canada's official languages - English and French.

But, although Mariko learns both Canadian and European French at l'Université Laval, we teach European accents of French because the examples available to us are clearer to students. Most French students want to go to France too.

I am also quick to point out orally and in writing, especially in special sessions I'm invited to offer outside of L.E.T.S., that there are 6,000 languages in the world.

I add that native speakers of English are fewer than 10% of the world population.

I advise people to study Chinese and Hindi before considering whether or not to study English, or French.

In Japan I also suggest that people study Korean, Chinese, and Russian because the closest neighbouring countries are Korea, China, and Russia.

With my writing skills added to Mariko's and her special knowledge and experience in language learning and teaching, she eventually writes a book about language learning that one of our sometimes* students describes as "amazingly honest". (*She comes to us when she has a very specific language need.)

Mariko's book describes the hard work required to learn and teach any language well and how to go about it.

She says her book is about how she learns a language and how she would like to be taught.

It's an adult learner's guide by an adult learner for other adult learners.

It's also a book by a professional adult educator to help other professional adult educators improve their approaches to adult learners.

ALIENATING EXPERIENCE

Mariko and I manage to get fairly open-ended visas in the U.K. enabling us to work there. The results are minimal and not lucrative.

We make two attempts to make the most of these visas. They bring us a couple of very low paying, short-term private adult students and a bit of interpreting work.

Only putting our names on a municipal "list of linguists" is somewhat helpful. It's a good idea and is referred to by the council office.

We also try to go through an agency that finds work for anyone. We go prepared with resumes showing our education and extensive experience abroad.

The response is unexpected.

Instead of thinking about how such an advanced and varied background could be useful in the U.K., the desk agent practically shrugs and only says:

"Let us know when you get some U.K. experience." How?

Adult educators with outside experience are of no interest to this European country?

We try another agency and, months after we leave the U.K., one of Mariko's references says he gets a request from a U.K. organization. Too late.

INSIDER TRADE?

Having, but not having the course

We're always interested in teaching local adult learners in Canada and bringing students here just as we do in Ottawa, Québec City, and Gatineau.

But Dyingtown is slave labour compared with Nippon.

The only place in Canada where we could have an income comparable to Nippon for comparable effort would be in Ottawa-Gatineau by working on contracts for a government bureaucracy.

But those opportunities are restricted. Contracts seem to be awarded to laid-off bureaucrats who set up private training firms, according to our contacts inside the government.

It may simply be a way that governments take one type of spending off the financial books and file it somewhere else.

Or there might be some real money saving, although private companies, unlike governments, want to make financial profits.

It's reminiscent of removing certain products and services from the annual inflation statistics to create the illusion that inflation is very low instead of much higher for people who do the daily shopping.

Whatever the case, we're not on the insiders' track for getting government contracts or posts in adult education.

LINGUISTICS & LANGUAGE TEACHING MAJORS NEED NOT APPLY

This volume concludes with a very short story about the time Mariko and I are invited to visit an Ottawa area non-profit organization offering official language classes to newcomers to Canada.

We would like to cooperate with the organization.

During most of our visit we are sitting with a group of students listening to people running the organization talking about how it works and how it helps people learn.

After all the talk I approach one of the organizers.

She tells us that the first thing she has to know about any teachers working with them is whether or not they have TESOL certification.

She says teachers need to have university degrees in TESOL, not the six month certificates that people get so they can have jobs overseas.

She makes no mention of language training and linguistics studies and degrees. So I ask her point blank:

"Are you saying that someone with a PhD in language teaching or linguistics can't work with you?"

She replies, "You'll have to check with TESOL."

This gives me an even greater appreciation of Dr. Verner's opposition of "certification". It excludes very qualified, competent, and widely-experienced adult educators like Mariko.

TESOL is evidently the supreme being of the Ottawa group we visit.

It's their loss, not ours.

Unfortunately, it's also a loss for the taxpayers enabling the group to have non-profit status.

Unfortunately, it's also a loss for the newcomers to Canada who go to the non-profit organization in the hope of getting the best available language training that it can provide.

Here again is an example of an organization with a very narrow, top-down approach to adult education.

For the non-profit group, TESOL rules in the same absolute manner as the way that schooling systems rule adult night school as if they were merely extensions of child/adolescent schooling.

For the non-profit group, if it's not TESOL certified, it's not real language education.

And the certificate is not the end of it.

The TESOL certified must also become members of TESOL and pay the organization annual dues.

Yet TESOL does not appear to be involved in contract negotiations with employers, unlike a trade union or professional organization.

For employers, TESOL is apparently no more than a "recognized" seal of approval to simplify the work of personnel departments staffed by people with no knowledge of professional language education.

Adult language teachers and linguistics with university degrees in their fields need not apply.

This is yet another example of "our way or the highway".

This encounter with the true believers of certification also gives me a deeper appreciation of Dr. Verner's opposition to the certification of professional adult educators, no matter what they teach.

People dabbling in adult education, such as professional school teachers in night school (with inappropriate teaching certificates) and L.B.E. staff with no qualifications except their tongues, do not advance adult education.

But attempting to hamstring and limit the supply of adult educators through an exaggerated devotion to certification, (particularly when its only one form of certification), is not an appropriate, acceptable, or desirable means of helping more adult learners to learn more.

L.E.T.S. & Adult Education

As mentioned earlier, Mariko and I invent our own, very small adult education organization, applying the most flexible approach possible to help adult learners.

We offer our services as adult educators in a manner that no type of educational organization or business offers and/or can offer these services.

They are too obsessed with habit, security, and/or bookkeeping going far beyond balancing their budgets.

It's not always only because their prime interest is in fulfilling a role mandated by government legislation or the benevolent dictates of philanthropic private funding, and the strict or fixed annual budgets of such organizations.

It's not only because they are, like the language business establishments and similar companies, only interested in making the maximum profit for the minimum cost to themselves, minimum customer services, and/or minimum investment, and such organizations' lack the knowledge, training, and commitment to learning possessed by professional educators.

In theory, they could do exactly what we are doing while fulfilling their mandates and making financial profits.

But in practice they are too consumed with doing things in what they devoutly believe are the long time-tested and trusted approaches of all eternity before now.

They are repeating, by rote memory, all of the familiar behaviours, like the school boards' rigid night school approach of re-schooling adults; and following a business model to its predictable positive income outcomes of traditional business planning and accounting.

They are too cumbersome, big, and/or bureaucratic to do what we do. They can hardly imagine trying to do what we are doing.

They lack our interest and dedication because their organizations constantly mitigate against applying theirs as fully as we can apply ours.

That's because we are dedicated entirely and solely to helping adult learners to learn. It isn't just a job or a business. It's what we do.

We aren't out to make money, but the money comes anyway because the adult learners who want our services know they can't get them anywhere else.

Of course they come to like us personally too and feel enthusiastic about studying with us because we stimulate their motivation to learn every time they come to us.

Although we don't work overnight like Marvin's school, we are available to teach adult learners every day, including most statutory holidays, from early morning to mid-evening.

In our first years we have 36 courses every seven days. It's a busy time but we are not exhausted. We arrange a break after and before each class.

We always prepare for classes in advance and insist that each learner does the same thing if s/he wants to remain with us.

We have ample time to eat our meals and we can often watch several video recordings of motion pictures between classes.

We can socialize and take walks too. During our busiest years, Mariko goes to a nearby gymnasium almost every day to take aerobics classes too.

Most learners come to us individually and most others arrive in small groups of colleagues or friends.

So, with our help, learners can easily change the days and times of their courses at any time. All they have to do is phone us to arrange changes.

The only restriction we impose is that courses be arranged in about 30-day packages, and all courses in a package must be completed within the 30 days.

Their course content is based on themselves, their lives and needs, including the reason they want to learn, even if it's basically a strong interest, like a model train collector.

We ask them to tell us as much as they can about their homes, their families, their work; their friends; their love lives; their travel plans.

Their courses change as we learn more about the learners, i.e. things they don't mention or forget when we start the courses.

We create and produce very simple audio, video, and other course material based entirely upon what they are teaching us about themselves.

Nothing is "off-the-rack", "canned", or otherwise available for sale anywhere. Our students buy nothing. They only pay course tuition.

We don't sell our students anything. We consider the materials that we create and produce are merely part of the courses, not merchandise.

Unlike businesses, we don't charge any student an "admission fee".

Our students are free to quit their courses at any time. They can tell us they are quitting on the day of the last class that they are taking.

Our students rarely quit and we rarely tell them to quit.

We tell each learner before s/he begins studying with us that if s/he studies s/he can have a very enjoyable time and increase the probability that s/he will learn a great deal.

We also tell each learner before s/he begins studying with us that if s/he does not study, s/he and we will suffer, make no progress, and waste our time together.

We warn her/him that we will cancel the course and no longer accept them as our students.

We tell every potential learner who is interested in coming to us that such a poor outcome is a waste of an adult learner's money and a waste of an adult educator's teaching skills.

It is mutually unbeneficial. We aren't interested in this outcome.

Again, for us adult education isn't about taking money from other people.

It's only about helping them to learn and making them and ourselves feel good about this accomplishment.

In the process, our lives become richer because we are constantly learning something we don't know from the great variety of adult learners who choose to study with us.

As a by-product, we are continuing to live and replenish ourselves, while paying for our housing, food, and minimalist adventurous lives.

Adult education makes everyone's life better.

Adult education is inextricably linked to and dependent upon the ongoing leadership and direction of adult learners.

Adult education is not something imposed upon adult learners by others.

The failures and successes of adult education endeavours depend on the adult learners and their participation in determining and designing their own courses.

Making up and overwhelming adult learners with hundreds or thousands of courses is not participation. It is domination and manipulation.

VOLUMES FROM MYTHBREAKER
Terrian Journals series:
A Sketch of Terrian History
Terrian Journals' How To Make The Nation
Full Employment: Not Fulfilling
Terrian
Terrian Journals: Living as a Newcomer
Middle Earth Journals
Rediscovery Journals
Fukurokuju No Kasumi Journals
Sabbatical Journals
Departure Journals
Adventuredate Unknown Journals
Away Team Journals
Searching For South Journals
Inonakanokawazu Journals
КАЗАНЬ Journals
Terrian Journals for the Misguided
Terrian Journals' N.S.R.: Not Spying, …Really!
TJ JNG: Terrian Journals' Jokes Nobody Gets
Terrian Journals' Miss Schooling?
Terrian Journals' Disbelief
Terrian Journals' House Trap
Terrian Journals' Virtually Camping
Terrian Journals' Crystal
Virtually Dead
Terrian Journals' Maximum Insecurity
Terrian Journals First Anthology
Terrian Journals Second Anthology

Archway series:
Archway: Six Year Book of Dreams
Archway: Lifetime Rhyme
Archway's Valentine Love
Archway's Garden Rhymes
Archway's Christmas New Years Rhymes
Archway Life Before Dreams

Additional Titles:
Language Learning Secrets
Trying To Teach Languages In The L.B.E. World
An Adult Book About Education

www.ingramcontent.com/pod-product-compliance
Lightning Source LLC
Chambersburg PA
CBHW060152050426
42446CB00013B/2777